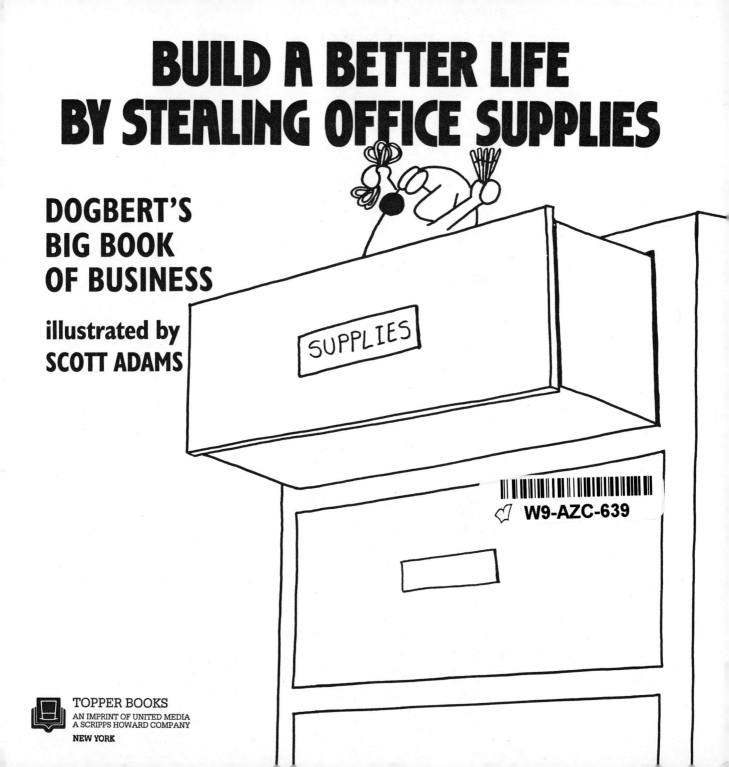

For the twentieth of every month

First published in 1991

Library of Congress Cataloging-in-Publication Data
Adams, Scott.
Build a better life by stealing office supplies:
Dogbert's big book of business / illustrated by Scott Adams.
p. cm.
ISBN 0-88687-637-0 : $7.95
I. Title
PN6727.A3B85   1991
745.5'973—dc20

Topper Books
An imprint of United Media
A Scripps Howard Company
200 Park Avenue
New York, NY 10166

10 9 8 7 6

Topper Books are available at special discounts on bulk purchases for
sales promotions, premiums, fundraising or educational use. For details,
contact the Special Sales Department, St. Martin's Press, 175 Fifth Avenue,
New York, NY 10010 or call 1-800-221-7945.

Dogbert and Dilbert appear regularly in their own comic strip, DILBERT™, made available to your hometown paper, college newspaper, or business newsletter by the fine folks at United Feature Syndicate.

CONTENTS

FOREWORD by Dogbert

Many pompous business books have been written in the last few years. This is another one. But unlike its predecessors, this book offers practical information.

Other business books have offered such useful insights as "profitable companies pay high salaries." What exactly are we supposed to do with that kind of information? Should unprofitable companies raise salaries to become more profitable?

Let's face it, companies that are profitable are usually in the right place at the right time, and that's all there is to it. Those companies could be managed by gerbils and they would still make money hand over paw. Sure, in the beginning somebody invented something valuable, or stole it from somebody else, but since then it's been strictly auto-pilot.

So forget about making the company more profitable; it's out of your control. Put your energy where it will make the most difference: surviving your frustrating and thankless job.

What the world needs is a practical guide to business—one which the average white collar worker can understand and use. That's why I wrote **Dogbert's Big Book of Business**. That's why it has simple cartoon pictures.

To research this book I spent nearly two weeks working at a large American company. This was long enough to become an expert by American standards, but not so long that the life force would be sucked out of me.

I hope you enjoy my book.

DRESSING FOR SUCCESS

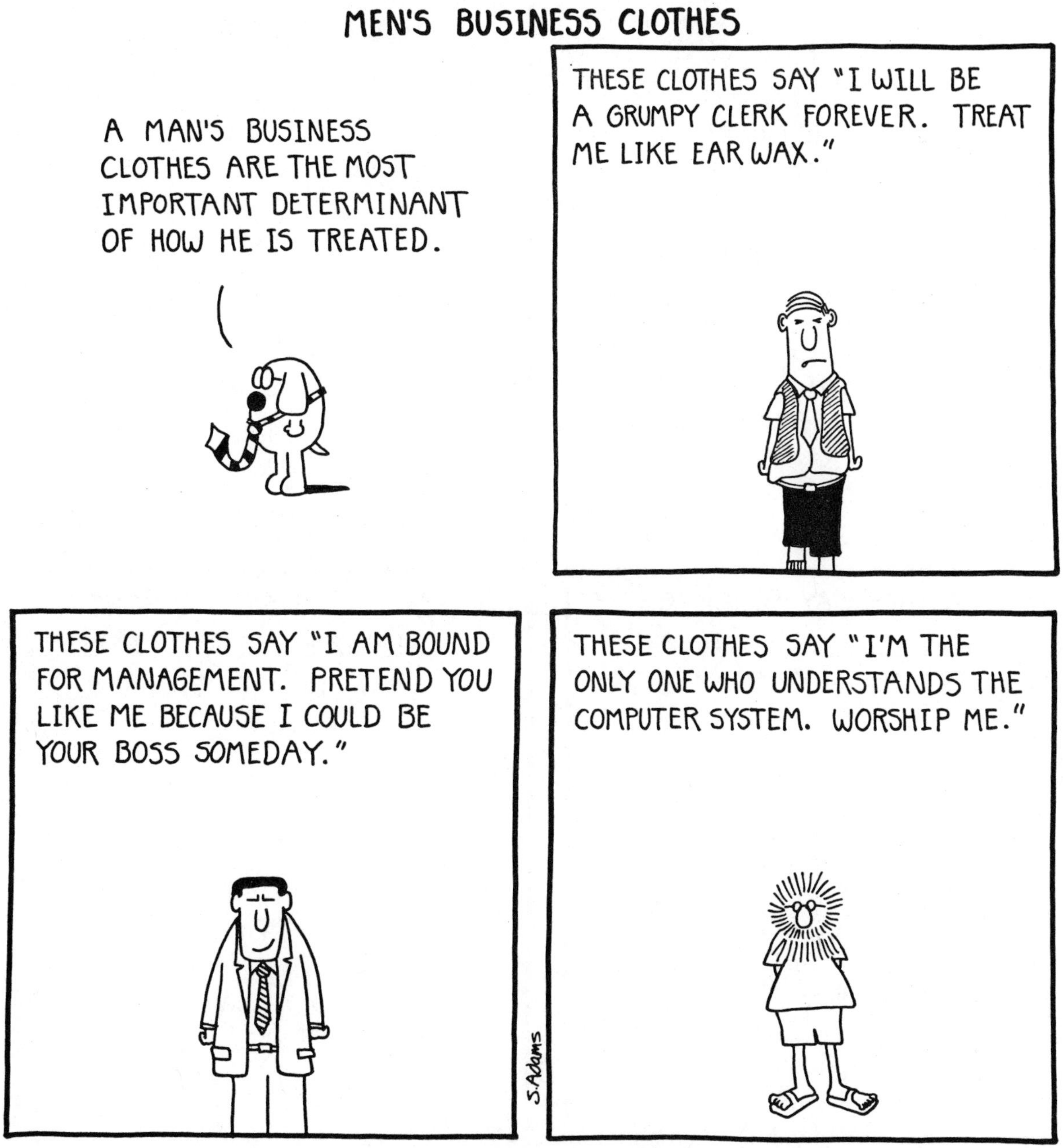
MEN'S BUSINESS CLOTHES
A MAN'S BUSINESS CLOTHES ARE THE MOST IMPORTANT DETERMINANT OF HOW HE IS TREATED.
THESE CLOTHES SAY "I WILL BE A GRUMPY CLERK FOREVER. TREAT ME LIKE EAR WAX."
THESE CLOTHES SAY "I AM BOUND FOR MANAGEMENT. PRETEND YOU LIKE ME BECAUSE I COULD BE YOUR BOSS SOMEDAY."
S.Adams
THESE CLOTHES SAY "I'M THE ONLY ONE WHO UNDERSTANDS THE COMPUTER SYSTEM. WORSHIP ME."

WOMEN'S BUSINESS CLOTHES

WOMEN UNDERSTAND HOW TO USE BUSINESS CLOTHES TO CONVEY SUBTLE MESSAGES.

THESE CLOTHES SAY "I LIKE EATING CHOCOLATE MORE THAN I LIKE THIS STUPID JOB."

THESE CLOTHES SAY "I AM A SUCCESSFUL BUSINESS WOMAN. GET OUT OF MY WAY, DAMN IT."

THESE CLOTHES SAY "I HOPE YOU WILL IGNORE THE STUFF THAT COMES OUT OF MY MOUTH."

S. Adams

STAINS

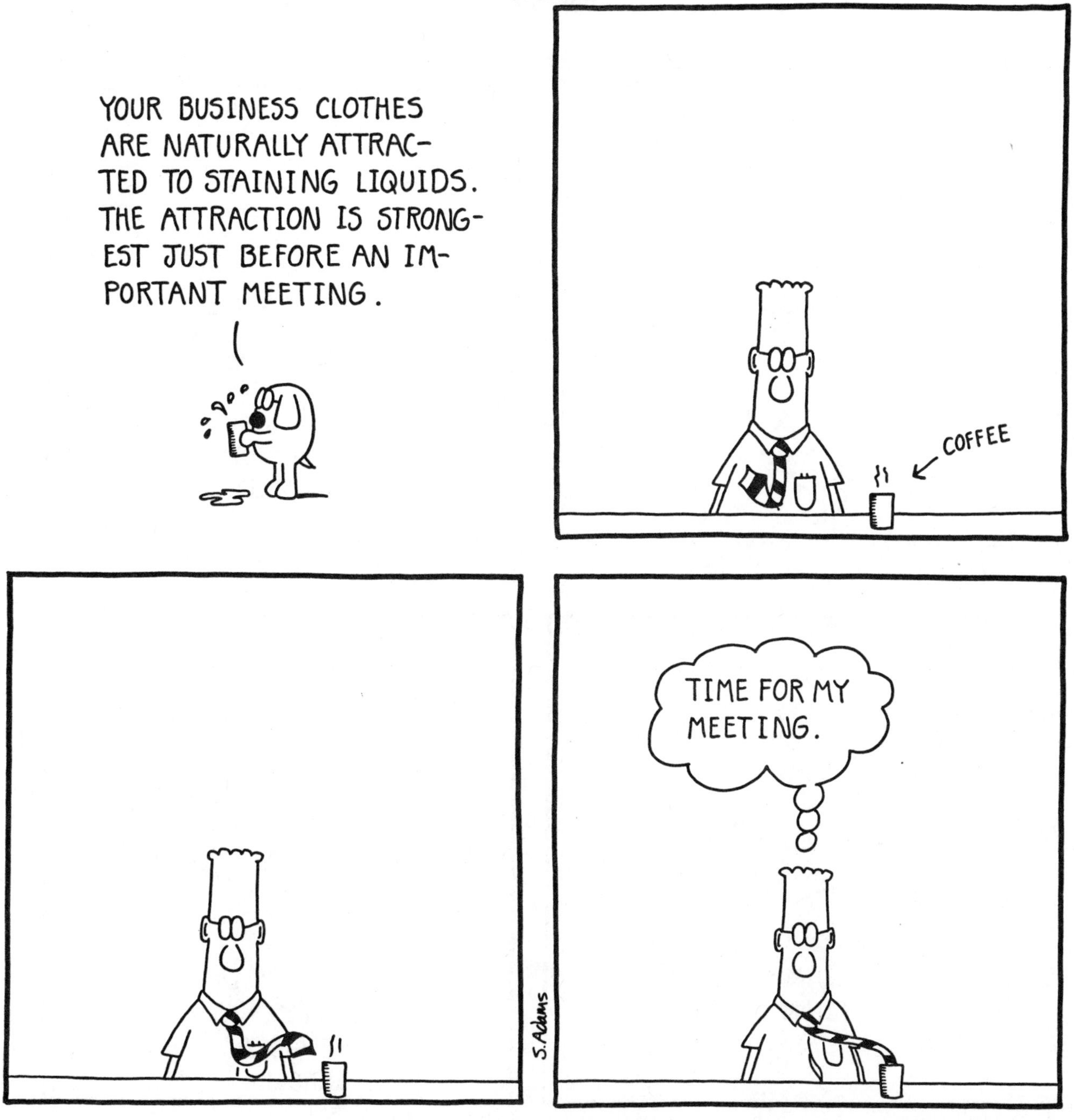
YOUR BUSINESS CLOTHES ARE NATURALLY ATTRACTED TO STAINING LIQUIDS. THE ATTRACTION IS STRONGEST JUST BEFORE AN IMPORTANT MEETING.
COFFEE
S. Adams
TIME FOR MY MEETING.

BUSINESS ETIQUETTE

THE POWER HANDSHAKE

YOU CAN GAIN IMMEDIATE DOMINANCE IN A BUSINESS SITUATION BY FORCING THE OTHER PERSON TO SHAKE HANDS LIKE A PATHETIC WIMP.

APPROACH NORMALLY

CLAMP THEIR FINGERTIPS

SHAKE THEIR HELPLESS HAND LIKE A DEAD SPARROW

HALLWAY ETIQUETTE

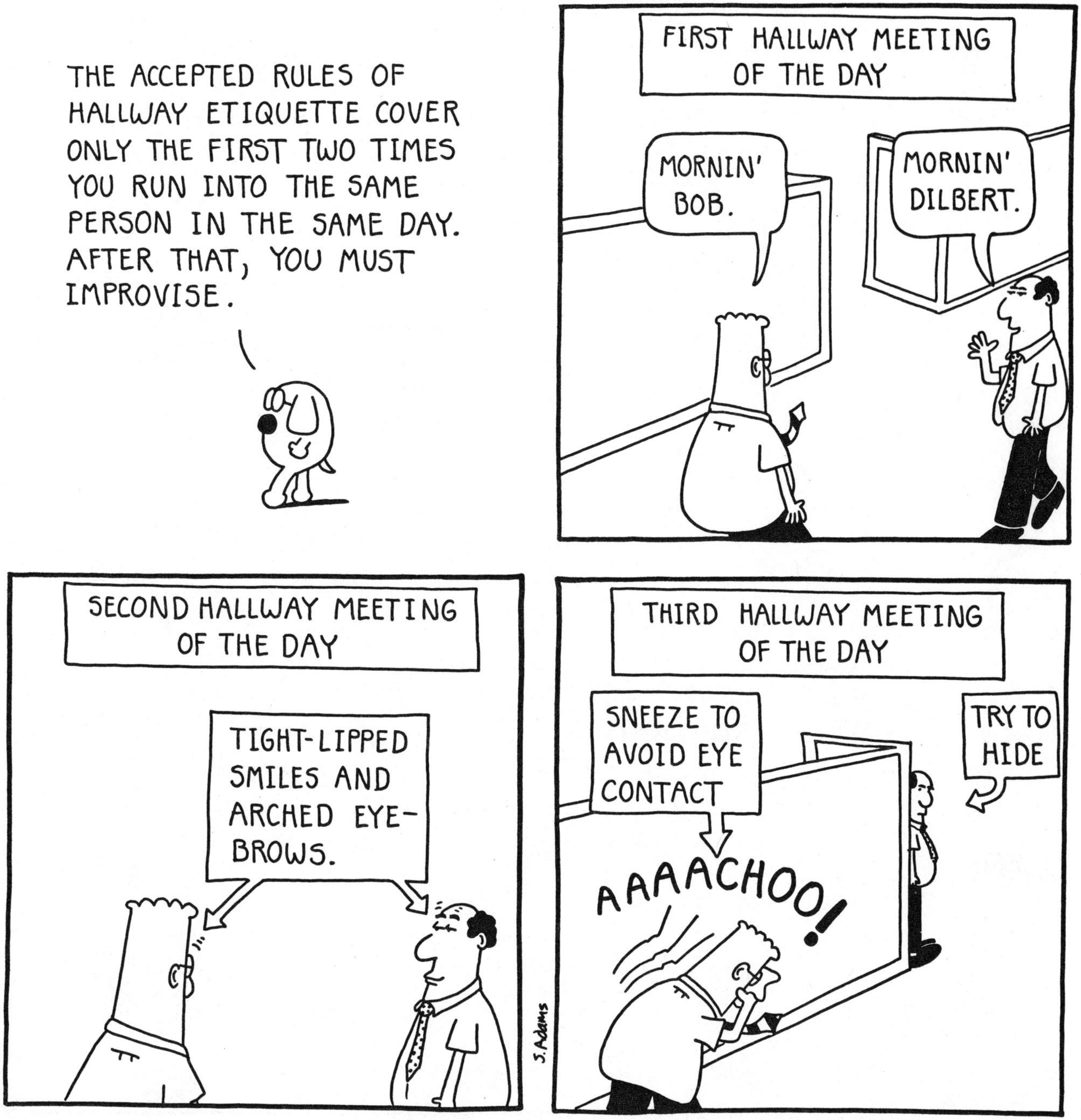
THE ACCEPTED RULES OF HALLWAY ETIQUETTE COVER ONLY THE FIRST TWO TIMES YOU RUN INTO THE SAME PERSON IN THE SAME DAY. AFTER THAT, YOU MUST IMPROVISE.
FIRST HALLWAY MEETING OF THE DAY
MORNIN' BOB.
MORNIN' DILBERT.
SECOND HALLWAY MEETING OF THE DAY
TIGHT-LIPPED SMILES AND ARCHED EYE-BROWS.
S. Adams
THIRD HALLWAY MEETING OF THE DAY
SNEEZE TO AVOID EYE CONTACT
TRY TO HIDE
AAAACHOO!

SALARY ETIQUETTE

IT IS CONSIDERED IMPOLITE TO ASK CO-WORKERS THEIR SALARIES; HOWEVER, IT IS PERFECTLY ACCEPTABLE TO DEDUCE IT BY GRILLING THEM RELENTLESSLY ON THEIR SPENDING HABITS.

DOGBERT'S LEISURE PERCEPTION PRINCIPLE

THE DOGBERT HARP

IF SOMEBODY MISSPEAKS AT A MEETING, IT IS YOUR OBLIGATION TO HARP ON IT OVER AND OVER AGAIN.

...AND GROSS SALES ARE DOWN TEN PERCENT THIS MONTH.

YOU MEAN <u>YEAR</u>, NOT MONTH.

TEN PERCENT THIS <u>MONTH</u>?!! IT'S IMPOSSIBLE. YOU HAVE LOST ALL CREDIBILITY. HOW CAN WE TRUST ANYTHING YOU SAY?!!

I MEANT "YEAR"... I MISSPOKE.

TEN PERCENT A <u>MONTH</u>?!! DO YOU TAKE US FOR IDIOTS?!!

PERSONAL PHONE CALLS

IF YOU HAVE A PERSONAL LIFE, LET EVERYBODY ENJOY IT. SIGNAL YOUR CO-WORKERS TO LISTEN TO YOUR PERSONAL CALLS BY CHANGING YOUR POSTURE AND LOWERING YOUR VOICE.

OFFICE POLITICS

DEMAGOGUERY

ONE SURE WAY TO THE TOP IS TO INVENT SCAPEGOATS IN THE COMPANY AND LEAD THE CHARGE AGAINST THEM. IDEALLY, THE SCAPEGOATS SHOULD BE POWERLESS AND FUNNY LOOKING.

I HAVE TRACED THE SOURCE OF OUR DECLINING MARKET SHARE TO WILLY, OUR MAIL DELIVERY BOY.

WILLY MUST BE ELIMINATED, AND I MUST BE PROMOTED FOR SOLVING THE PROBLEM.

DEATH

S.Adams

DOGBERT'S LAUGHTER GUIDE

THE AMOUNT OF ENERGY
SPENT LAUGHING AT A
JOKE SHOULD BE DIRECTLY
PROPORTIONAL TO THE
HIERARCHICAL STATUS OF
THE JOKE TELLER.

LAUGHING AT YOUR BOSS'S JOKE

HEE HEE!
I'LL HAVE TO
REMEMBER
THAT.

YOUR BOSS'S BOSS'S JOKE.

HA HA HA !!
I'LL HAVE TO
WRITE THAT ONE
DOWN.

YOUR BOSS'S BOSS'S BOSS'S JOKE

HA HA HA
I'LL HAVE TO TATTOO THAT
ON MY BACK !!!

STAYING OUT OF TROUBLE

IT IS BETTER FOR YOUR CAREER TO DO NOTHING, THAN TO DO SOMETHING AND ATTRACT CRITICISM.

IT'S EERIE... HE'S BEEN STANDING MOTIONLESS LIKE THAT FOR DAYS.

HE MUST BE A FAST-TRACKER.

MAYBE I'VE UNDER-ESTI-MATED HIM.

S. Adams

OFFICE POLITICS

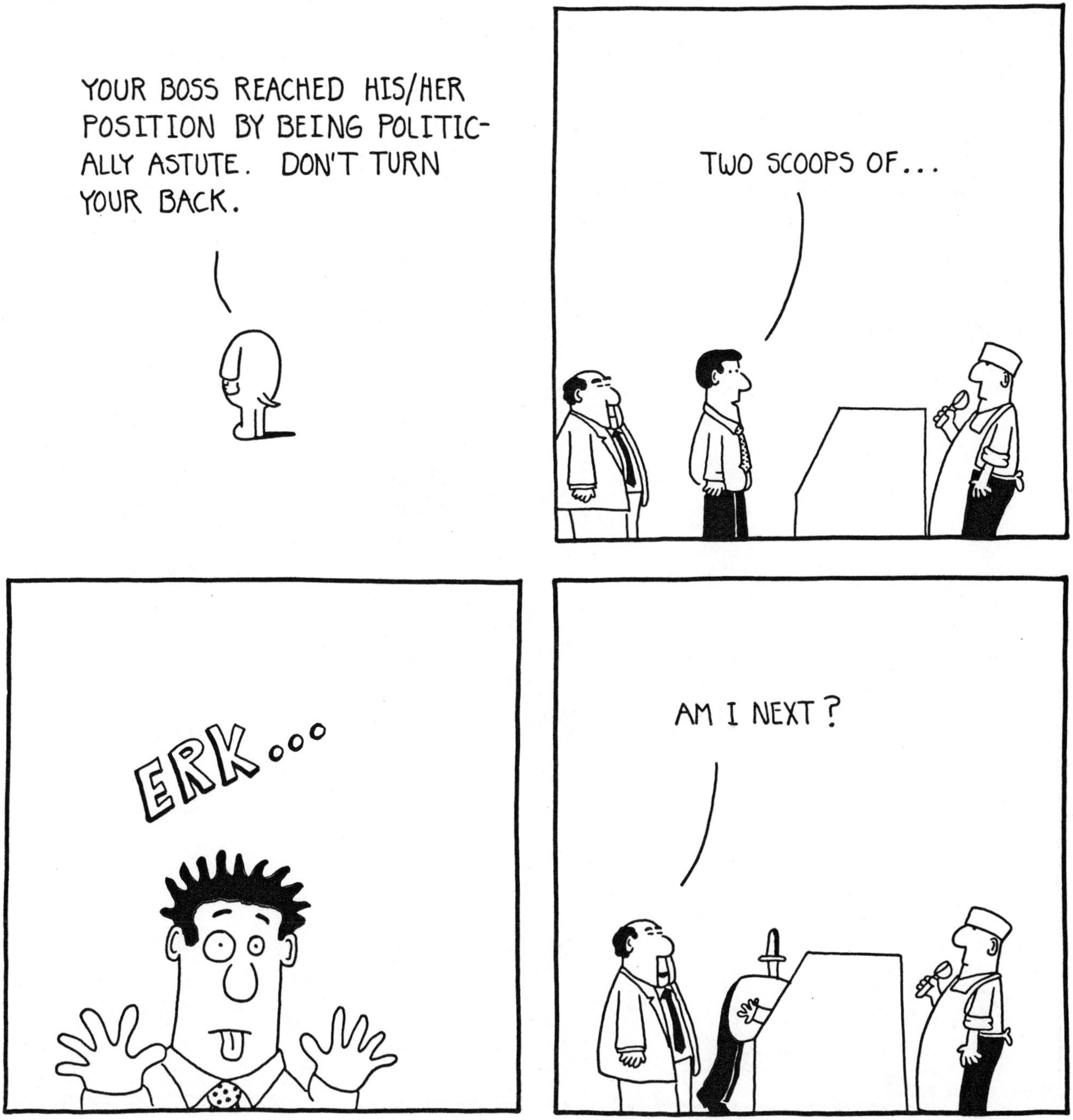
YOUR BOSS REACHED HIS/HER POSITION BY BEING POLITIC-ALLY ASTUTE. DON'T TURN YOUR BACK.
TWO SCOOPS OF...
ERK ooo
AM I NEXT?

TAKING CREDIT FOR OTHER PEOPLE'S WORK

IT IS MUCH EASIER TO TAKE CREDIT FOR OTHER PEOPLE'S WORK THAN TO DO YOUR OWN. GRAB EVERY OPPORTUNITY TO ASSOCIATE YOURSELF WITH PROJECTS WHICH ARE ALREADY SUCCESSFUL.

DE-POLITICIZING YOUR BUSINESS WRITING

BE CAREFUL THAT WHAT YOU WRITE DOES NOT OFFEND ANYBODY OR CAUSE PROBLEMS WITHIN THE COMPANY. THE SAFEST APPROACH IS TO REMOVE ALL USEFUL INFORMATION.

TAKE OUT THE DISCUSSION OF THE PROBLEM; IT COULD EMBARRASS SOMEBODY.

AND DON'T MENTION THE ALTERNATIVES; IT WILL JUST RAISE QUESTIONS.

OKAY, WHAT'S LEFT?

THE PAGE NUMBERS.

INEFFICIENCY AND YOUR CAREER

YOUR CAREER DEPENDS ON HOW MANY
PEOPLE WORK UNDER YOU. IT IS IN
YOUR BEST INTEREST TO INVOLVE AS
MANY PEOPLE AS POSSIBLE IN ANY
TASK. THAT WAY YOU CAN JUSTIFY
INCREASING YOUR STAFF.

KISSING UP

IF YOU HAVE NO SPECIAL TALENTS, AN UNGLAMOROUS METHOD IS AVAILABLE TO DISTINGUISH YOURSELF IN YOUR BOSS'S EYES.

CHANGE FOR THE SAKE OF PROMOTION

INSENSITIVITY: YOUR KEY TO MANAGEMENT SUCCESS

MONEY

CHANGES TO THE SALARY PLAN

ANY CHANGE TO THE SALARY PLAN WILL RESULT IN LESS MONEY FOR YOU. IF THEY WANTED TO GIVE YOU <u>MORE</u> MONEY, THEY WOULDN'T HAVE TO GO THROUGH ALL THE TROUBLE OF CHANGING THE PLAN.

YOUR SALARY

EVERY NIGHT, AFTER THE EMPLOYEES LEAVE, THE EXECUTIVES GET TOGETHER TO LAUGH ABOUT YOUR SALARIES.

WHAT MOTIVATES MANAGERS

FANTASY BUDGETING

NEVER BASE YOUR BUDGET REQUESTS ON REALISTIC ASSUMPTIONS, AS THIS COULD LEAD TO A DECREASE IN YOUR FUNDING.

PLANNING YOUR BUDGET

THERE IS NO RELATIONSHIP BETWEEN YOUR ASSESSMENT OF YOUR BUDGET NEEDS AND WHAT YOU ACTUALLY RECEIVE.

THE GOOD MANAGEMENT PENALTY

IF YOU SPEND LESS THAN YOUR BUDGET, YOUR BUDGET WILL BE CUT THE FOLLOWING YEAR AS A PENALTY.

AS YOU CAN SEE, I'M FORTY PER-CENT UNDER BUDGET!

GOOD. I'M CUTTING YOUR BUDGET BY FORTY PERCENT.

THE CORRECT METHOD

I'M FORTY PERCENT OVER BUDGET.

I'LL JUST HAVE TO GIVE YOU MORE MONEY... DON'T LET THIS HAPPEN AGAIN!

S.ADAMS

MANAGEMENT SALARY INCENTIVES

THE BUREAUCRACY

GROUP WRITING

DOGBERT'S THEORY OF EMPLOYEE SUGGESTIONS

KNOWING THE ENEMY

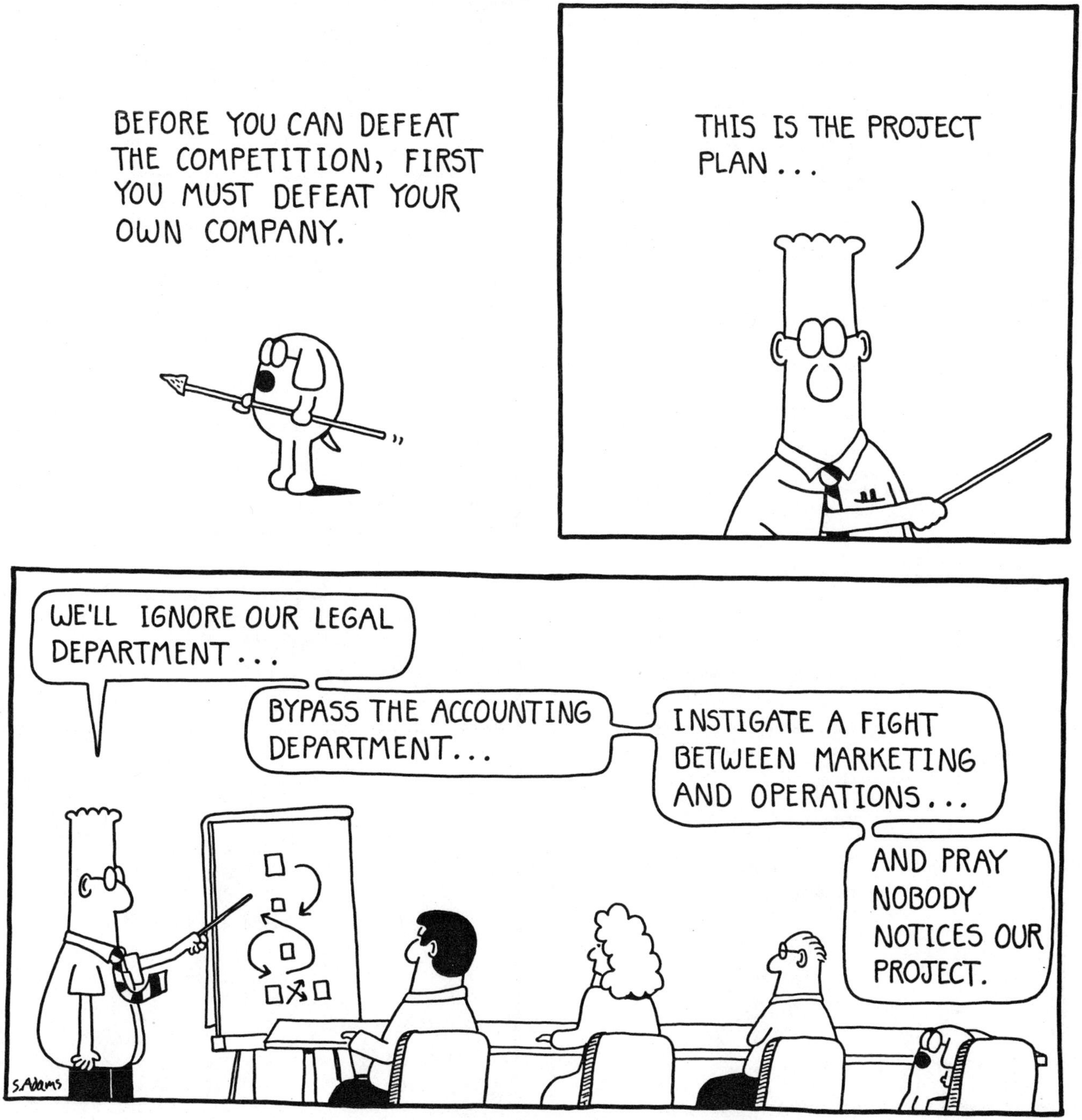
BEFORE YOU CAN DEFEAT THE COMPETITION, FIRST YOU MUST DEFEAT YOUR OWN COMPANY.
THIS IS THE PROJECT PLAN...
WE'LL IGNORE OUR LEGAL DEPARTMENT...
BYPASS THE ACCOUNTING DEPARTMENT...
INSTIGATE A FIGHT BETWEEN MARKETING AND OPERATIONS...
AND PRAY NOBODY NOTICES OUR PROJECT.
S. Adams

THE DOGBERT PHONE METHOD

FOLLOW THESE STEPS
TO GET RID OF CALLERS
WHO WANT INFORMATION.

1. NO MATTER WHAT THEY ASK, JUST GIVE THEM THE INFORMATION YOU HAVE RIGHT IN FRONT OF YOU.

I'VE GOT SOME GOOD INFORMATION ON THE DAYS OF THE WEEK . . .

2. IF THE CALLER PROTESTS, MAKE THEM RESTATE THE QUESTION. IN AS MANY FORMS AS POSSIBLE.

HOW WOULD THE HOPI INDIANS PHRASE THAT?

S. Adams

3. ACT LIKE THE CALLER'S QUESTION MAKES NO SENSE WHATSOEVER.

ARE YOU TALKING PIG LATIN? WHAT DO ALL OF THOSE WORDS MEAN?

CONTINUED...

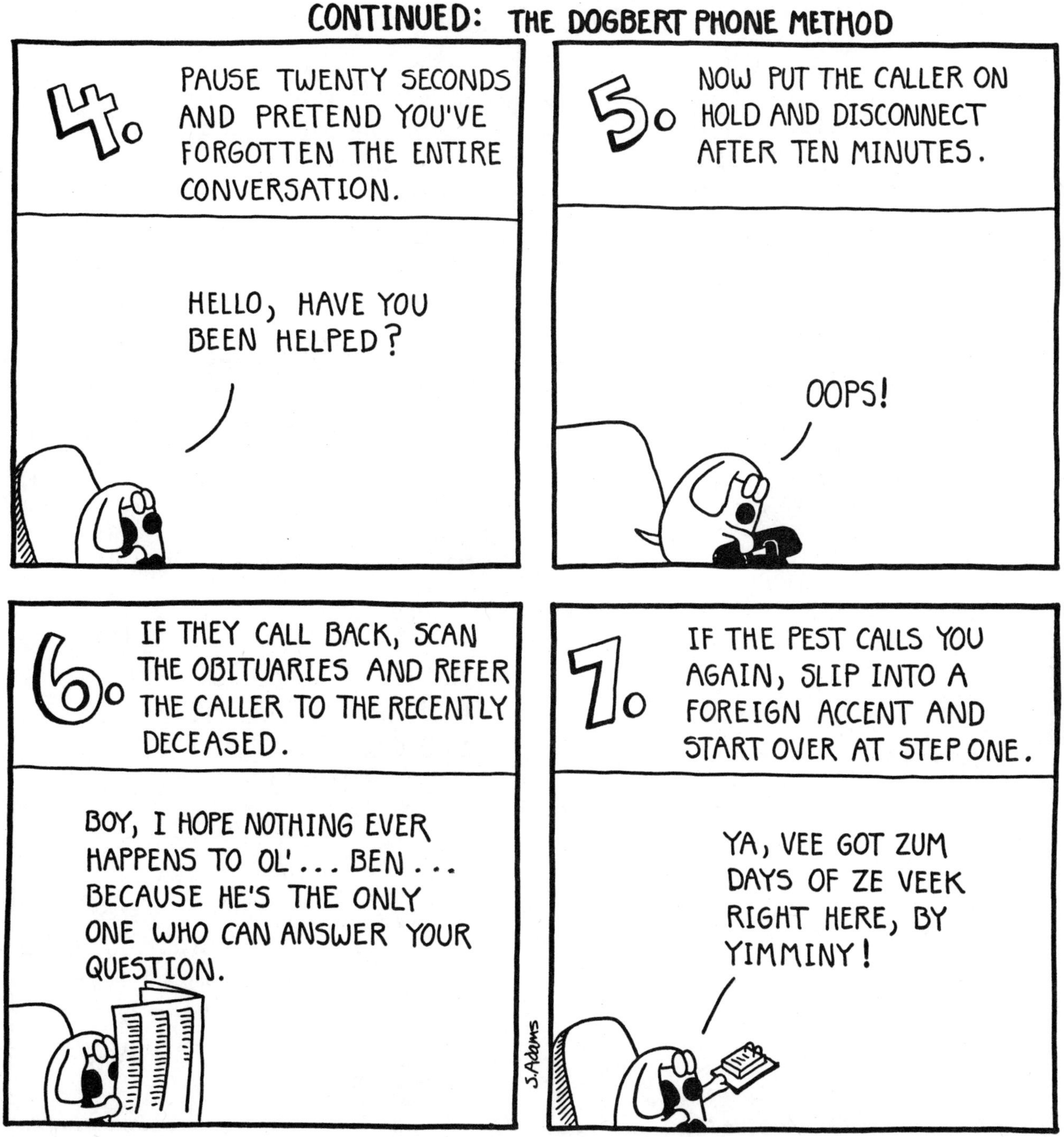
CONTINUED: THE DOGBERT PHONE METHOD
4. PAUSE TWENTY SECONDS AND PRETEND YOU'VE FORGOTTEN THE ENTIRE CONVERSATION.
HELLO, HAVE YOU BEEN HELPED?
5. NOW PUT THE CALLER ON HOLD AND DISCONNECT AFTER TEN MINUTES.
OOPS!
6. IF THEY CALL BACK, SCAN THE OBITUARIES AND REFER THE CALLER TO THE RECENTLY DECEASED.
BOY, I HOPE NOTHING EVER HAPPENS TO OL'... BEN... BECAUSE HE'S THE ONLY ONE WHO CAN ANSWER YOUR QUESTION.
7. IF THE PEST CALLS YOU AGAIN, SLIP INTO A FOREIGN ACCENT AND START OVER AT STEP ONE.
YA, VEE GOT ZUM DAYS OF ZE VEEK RIGHT HERE, BY YIMMINY!
S. Adams

THE DOGBERT SHUFFLE

YOUR PERCEIVED VALUE TO THE COMPANY IS DIRECTLY RELATED TO THE VOLUME OF PAPER YOU SHUFFLE. REQUEST COPIES OF ALL DOCUMENTS, NO MATTER HOW UNRELATED TO YOUR RESPONSIBILITIES.

DID YOU READ THE NEWSPAPER TODAY?

NO. CAN YOU MAKE A COPY FOR ME?

DO YOU WANT A COPY OF MY REPORT ON THE MEDICAL BENEFITS OF WAVING YOUR ARMS AROUND?

BETTER GIVE ME TWO — I'M DOUBLE-JOINTED.

YOU MIGHT NEED TO LOOK UP SOME OF THE MEDICAL TERMS IN THE DICTIONARY.

MAYBE YOU COULD RUN OFF A FEW COPIES OF THE DICTIONARY TOO.

S. Adams

DOGBERT'S PROJECT PLANNING FORMULA

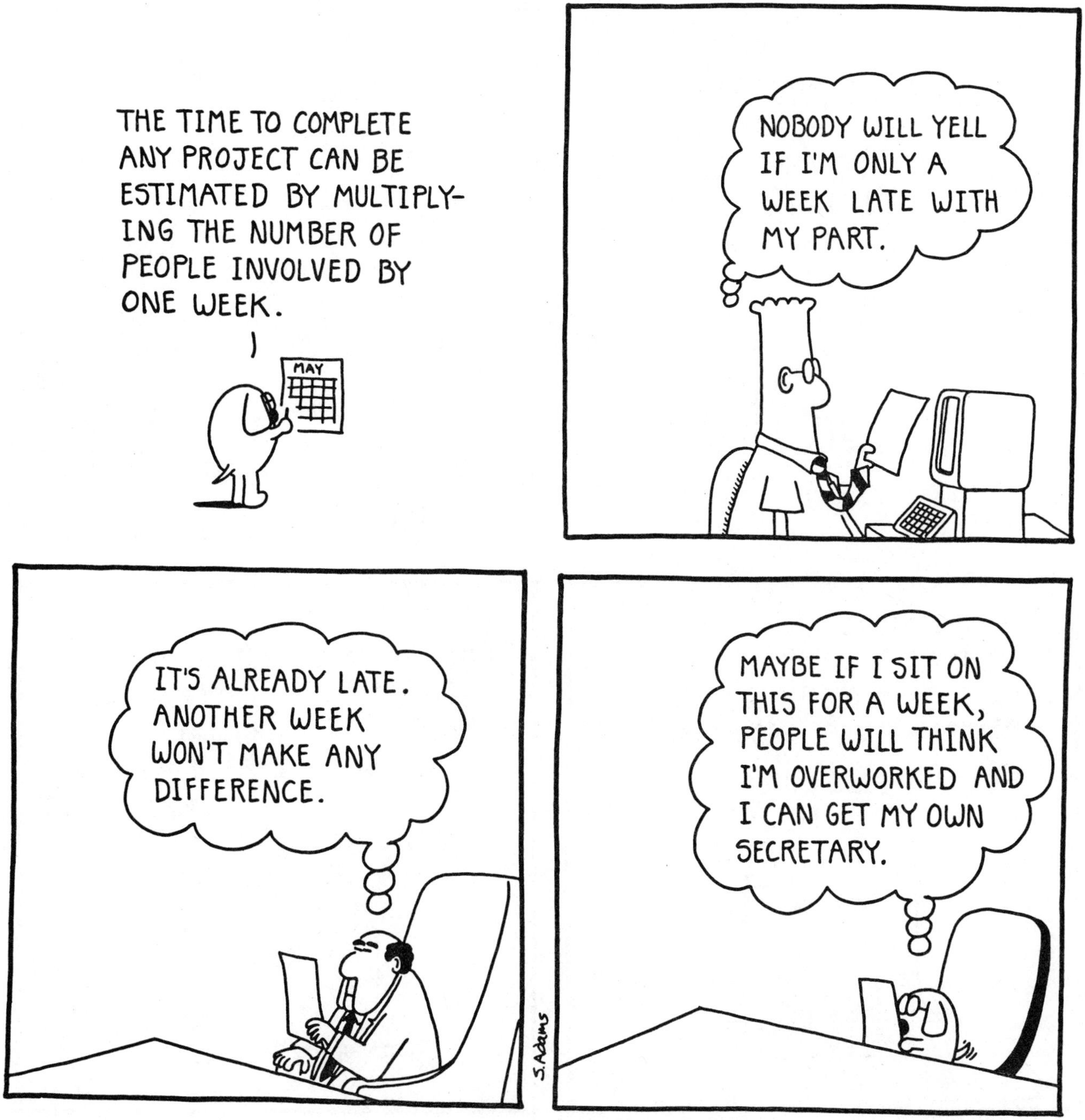
THE TIME TO COMPLETE ANY PROJECT CAN BE ESTIMATED BY MULTIPLYING THE NUMBER OF PEOPLE INVOLVED BY ONE WEEK.
MAY
NOBODY WILL YELL IF I'M ONLY A WEEK LATE WITH MY PART.
IT'S ALREADY LATE. ANOTHER WEEK WON'T MAKE ANY DIFFERENCE.
S. ADAMS
MAYBE IF I SIT ON THIS FOR A WEEK, PEOPLE WILL THINK I'M OVERWORKED AND I CAN GET MY OWN SECRETARY.

MAKING EXCEPTIONS

EXCEPTIONS MUST NEVER BE MADE; THEY ONLY LEAD TO WIDESPREAD EFFICIENCY AND A DIMINISHED NEED FOR PEOPLE IN YOUR JOB.

NO

I'M REQUESTING SEVEN DOLLARS FOR MY RESEARCH PROJECT.

WHAT? THERE'S NO COST-BENEFIT ANALYSIS ... NO EXTENSIVE DISCUSSION OF ALTERNATIVES... NO FINANCIAL ANALYSIS ...

THAT WOULD TAKE MONTHS, AND I'D HAVE TO MAKE UP MOST OF THE NUMBERS ...

IF YOU FOLLOW PROCEDURES, I WON'T HAVE TO RISK MAKING A DUMB DECISION.

S. Adams

DOGBERT'S LAW OF BUREAUCRATIC GRIDLOCK

THE ANSWER DEPENDS ON THE ASKER

NEVER ANSWER A QUESTION UNLESS YOU KNOW EXACTLY WHO IS ASKING, WHY IT IS BEING ASKED, AND WHAT WILL BE DONE WITH THE INFORMATION.

CAN I ASK YOU A QUESTION?

WHY DO YOU WANT TO KNOW? WHAT GROUP ARE YOU WITH? HOW WILL YOU USE THIS IN-FORMATION? ARE YOU GOING TO QUOTE ME? WHO ELSE ARE YOU TALKING TO? WHAT'S YOUR REAL MOTIVE HERE?

ACTUALLY, I JUST WANT DIRECTIONS TO THE MEN'S ROOM.

FOR YOUR OWN USE?

S.Adams

THE ADVANTAGE OF SMALL COMPANIES

BIG COMPANIES USE MOST OF THEIR RESOURCES TRYING TO KEEP PEOPLE FROM GETTING MAD AT THEM. SMALL COMPANIES HAVE MORE FLEXIBILITY.

MANAGEMENT BY SHAKING THE BOX

THE BENEFITS OF TITLE INFLATION

INFLATED JOB TITLES IN MIDDLE MANAGEMENT ALLOW THOSE AT THE BOTTOM OF THE COMPANY HIERARCHY TO AVOID TRULY DEMEANING TITLES.

PERFORMANCE AND PRODUCTIVITY

COFFEE PERFORMANCE GUIDE

YOUR HAPPINESS AND JOB PERFORMANCE ARE INFLU- ENCED MORE BY COFFEE THAN BY ANY OTHER FACTOR.

NO COFFEE

ONE CUP

TWO CUPS

THREE CUPS

FOUR CUPS

DOGBERT'S THEORY OF MONDAYS

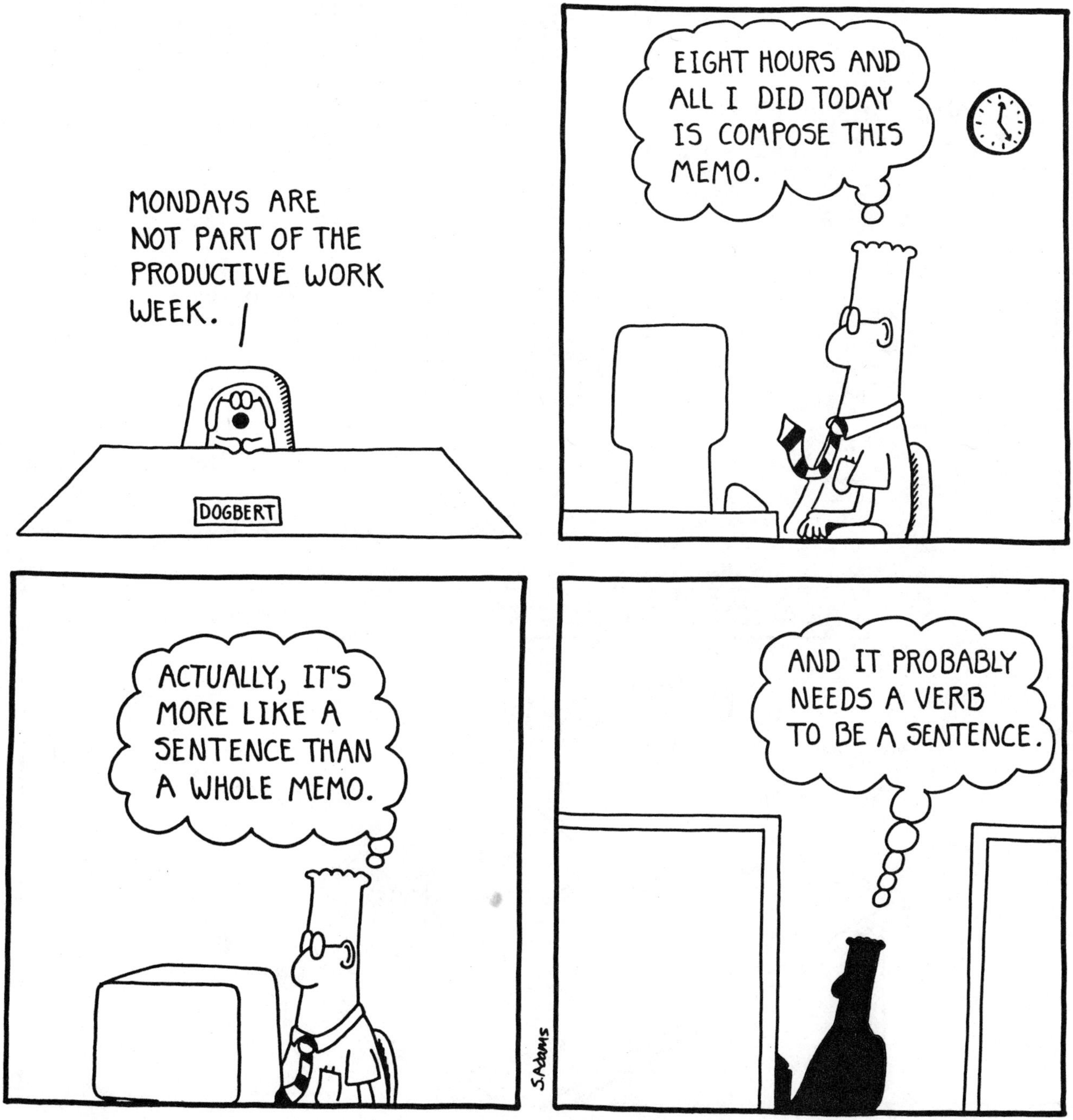

MONDAYS ARE NOT PART OF THE PRODUCTIVE WORK WEEK.
DOGBERT
EIGHT HOURS AND ALL I DID TODAY IS COMPOSE THIS MEMO.
ACTUALLY, IT'S MORE LIKE A SENTENCE THAN A WHOLE MEMO.
S.ADAMS
AND IT PROBABLY NEEDS A VERB TO BE A SENTENCE.

DOGBERT'S THEORY OF PERFORMANCE PERSPECTIVES

YOU AND YOUR BOSS WILL HAVE A DIFFERENT PERSPECTIVE ON YOUR PERFORMANCE.

CUBICLES

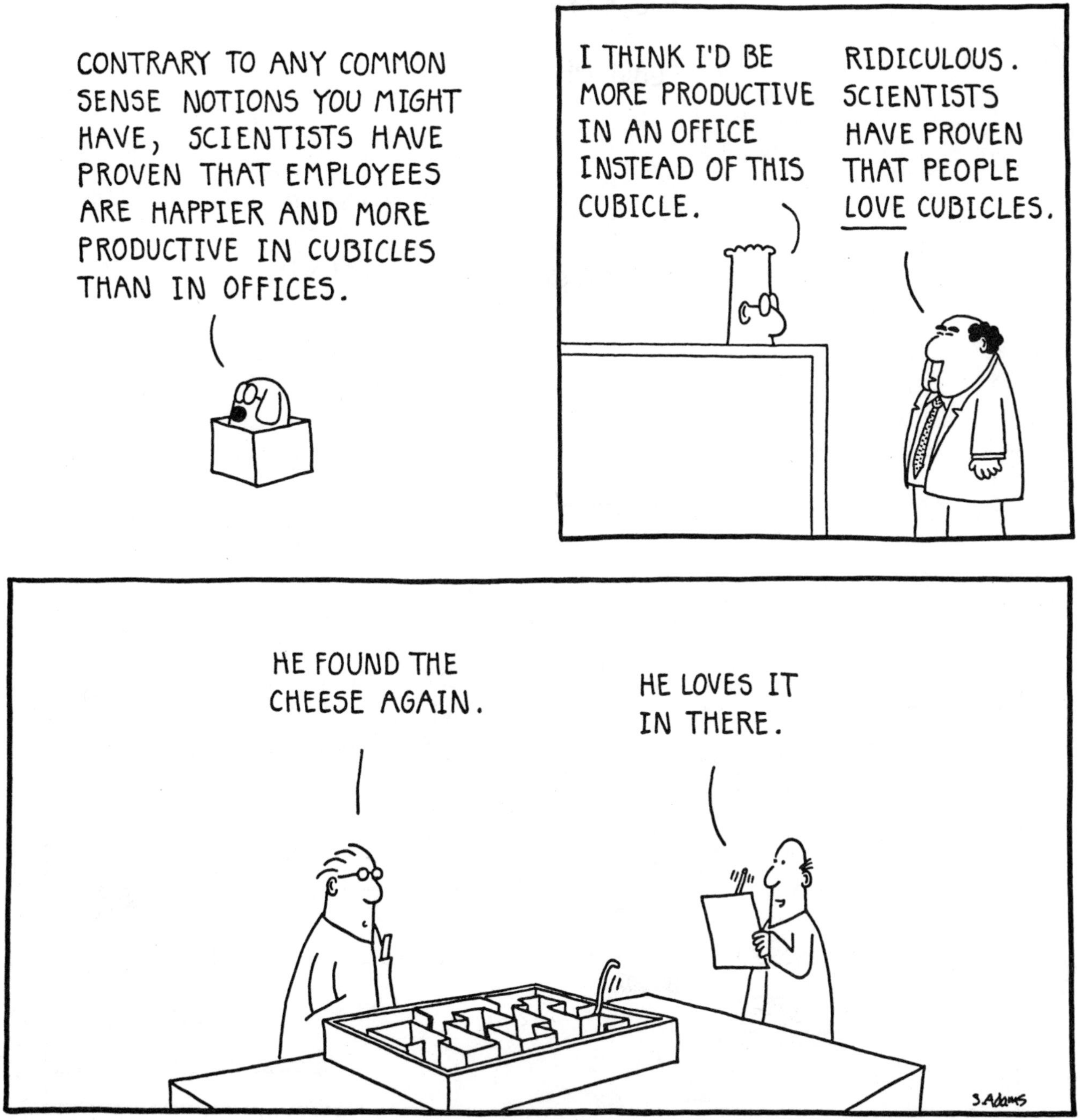
CONTRARY TO ANY COMMON SENSE NOTIONS YOU MIGHT HAVE, SCIENTISTS HAVE PROVEN THAT EMPLOYEES ARE HAPPIER AND MORE PRODUCTIVE IN CUBICLES THAN IN OFFICES.
I THINK I'D BE MORE PRODUCTIVE IN AN OFFICE INSTEAD OF THIS CUBICLE.
RIDICULOUS. SCIENTISTS HAVE PROVEN THAT PEOPLE LOVE CUBICLES.
HE FOUND THE CHEESE AGAIN.
HE LOVES IT IN THERE.
S.Adams

YOUR BOSS

LAW OF PROXIMITY

THE NEARER YOU ARE TO YOUR BOSS'S OFFICE, THE LOWER THE QUALITY OF YOUR ASSIGNMENTS.

BASIC MANAGEMENT TYPES

ALL MANAGERS FALL INTO ONE OF SEVERAL CATEGORIES. THE BEST YOU CAN HOPE IS TO HAVE A BOSS WHO DOESN'T NAUSEATE YOU OR KILL YOU.

MANAGEMENT STYLES (CONTINUED)

INSTRUCTIONS FROM THE BOSS

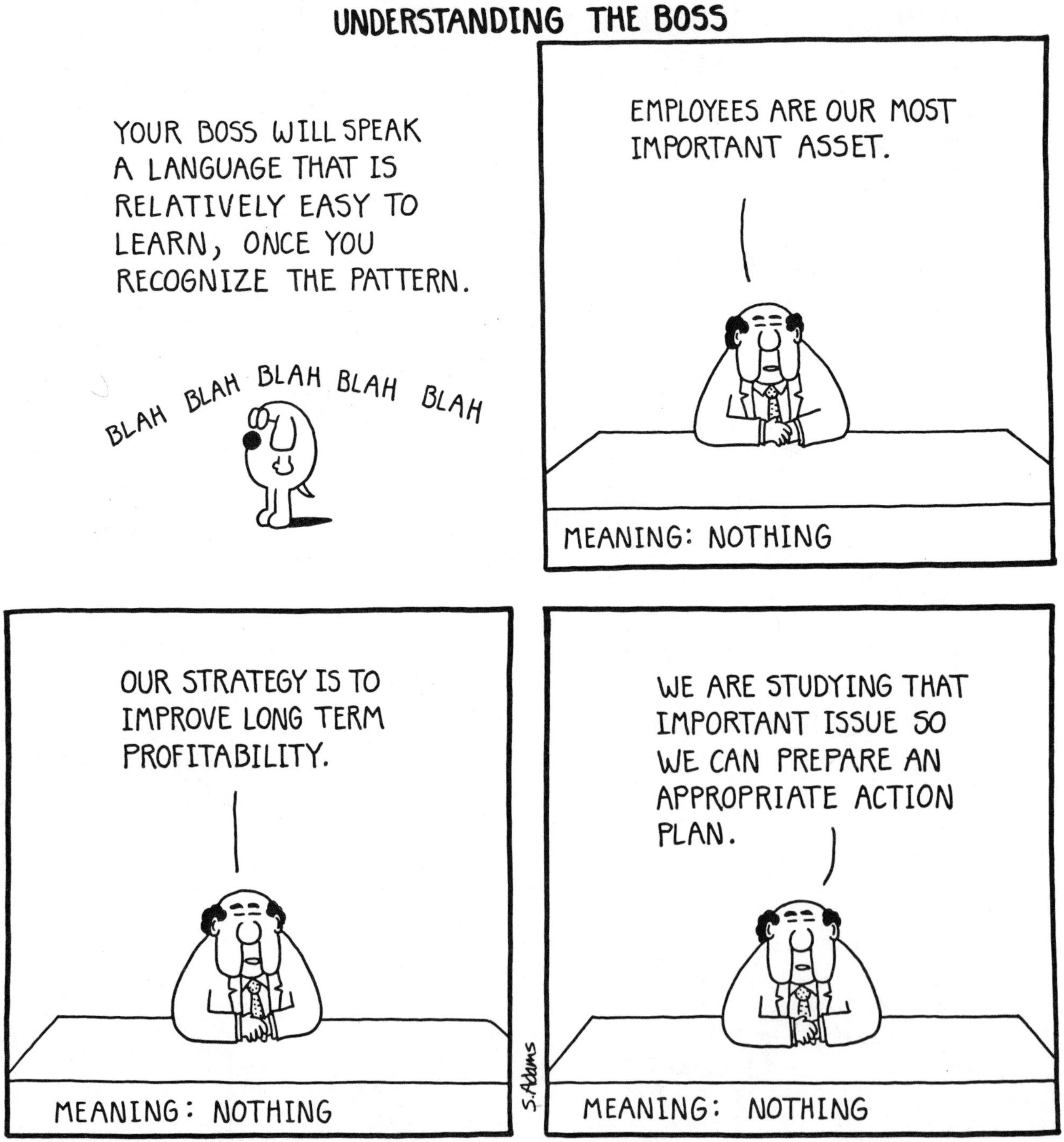
UNDERSTANDING THE BOSS
YOUR BOSS WILL SPEAK A LANGUAGE THAT IS RELATIVELY EASY TO LEARN, ONCE YOU RECOGNIZE THE PATTERN.
BLAH BLAH BLAH BLAH BLAH
EMPLOYEES ARE OUR MOST IMPORTANT ASSET.
MEANING: NOTHING
OUR STRATEGY IS TO IMPROVE LONG TERM PROFITABILITY.
MEANING: NOTHING
WE ARE STUDYING THAT IMPORTANT ISSUE SO WE CAN PREPARE AN APPROPRIATE ACTION PLAN.
MEANING: NOTHING
S. Adams

THE BIGGER THE BUILD-UP, THE WORSE THE ASSIGNMENT

KEEPING THE BOSS INFORMED

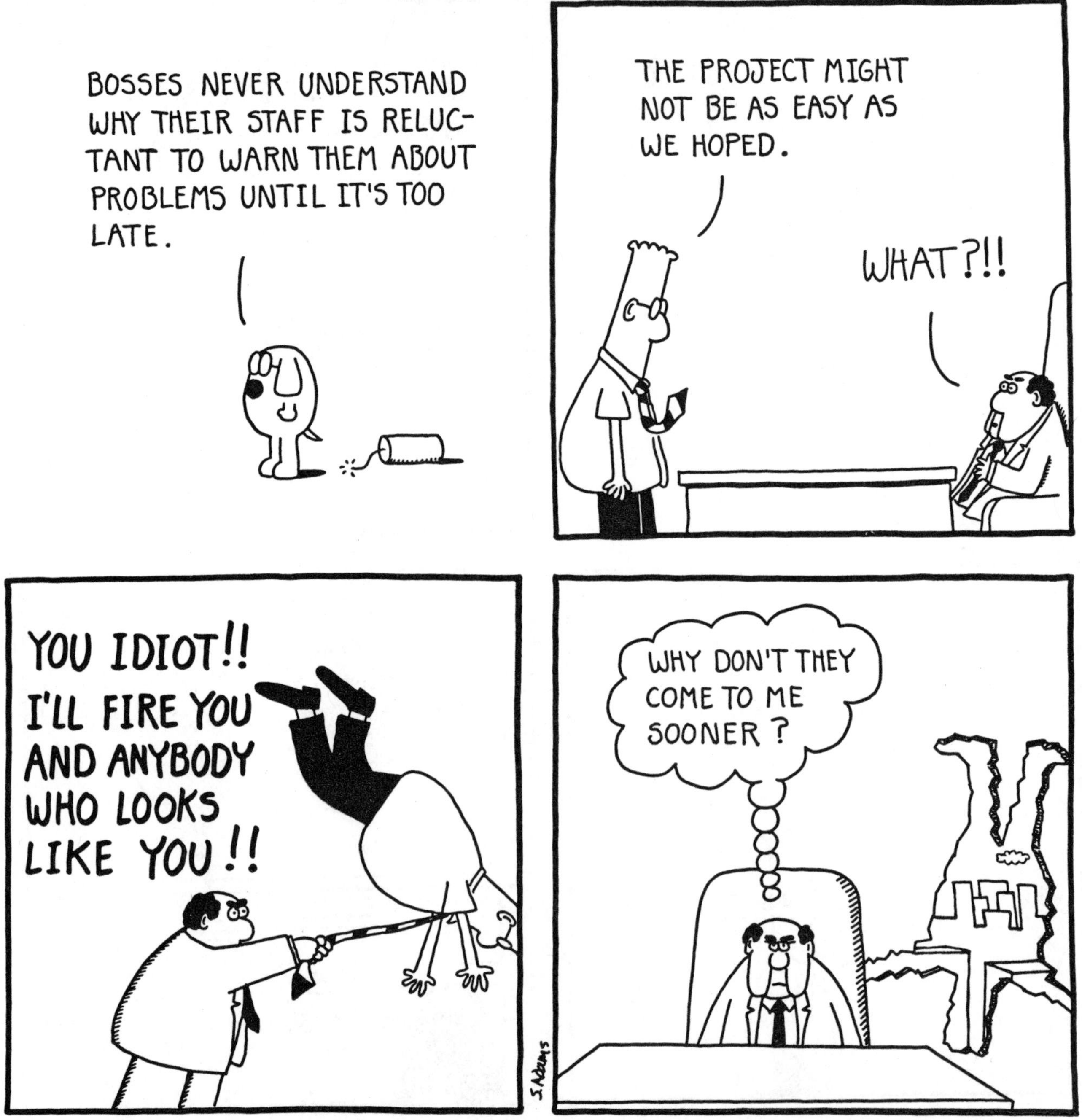
BOSSES NEVER UNDERSTAND WHY THEIR STAFF IS RELUCTANT TO WARN THEM ABOUT PROBLEMS UNTIL IT'S TOO LATE.
THE PROJECT MIGHT NOT BE AS EASY AS WE HOPED.
WHAT?!!
YOU IDIOT!! I'LL FIRE YOU AND ANYBODY WHO LOOKS LIKE YOU!!
WHY DON'T THEY COME TO ME SOONER?

READING BODY LANGUAGE

YOU CAN TELL WHAT YOUR BOSS IS THINKING BY LEARNING TO READ THE SUBTLE, UNCONSCIOUS SIGNALS OF HIS/HER BODY.

THIS POSITION SAYS "I AM NOT OPEN TO YOUR SUGGESTION."

THIS POSITION SAYS "I AM NOT LISTENING TO YOUR SUGGESTION."

♫ Oh when the saints go marching in... da da da ♫

THIS POSITION SAYS "YOU HAVE REPEATED YOUR SUGGESTION TOO MANY TIMES."

S. Adams

PERFORMANCE APPRAISALS

IF A MIRACLE OCCURS AND YOUR BOSS ACTUALLY COMPLETES YOUR PERFORMANCE APPRAISAL, IT WILL BE HASTILY PREPARED, ANNOYINGLY VAGUE, AND AN INSULT TO WHATEVER DIGNITY YOU MIGHT STILL POSSESS.

CO-WORKERS

SUFFERING FOOLS

AS YOU SUSPECTED, ALL OF YOUR
CO-WORKERS ARE FOOLS. YOU MUST
LEARN TO PITY AND TOLERATE
THEM.

DATING CO-WORKERS

THE WORLD IS FULL OF ATTRACT- IVE PEOPLE WHOM YOU WILL NEVER MEET. YOUR ONLY HOPE FOR ROMANCE IS TO LOWER YOUR STANDARDS UNTIL CO-WORKERS LOOK GOOD.

YOU KNOW, WHEN I STARTED HERE, I THOUGHT YOU WERE A COMPLETE LOSER.

BUT NOW I ONLY THINK YOU'RE A SEVEN-EIGHTHS LOSER.

WHEN SHE GETS DOWN TO FIVE-EIGHTHS I'LL MAKE MY MOVE.

S. Adams

THE BOSS'S SECRETARY

THE MOST PERILOUS CHALLENGE YOU WILL EVER FACE IS DEALING WITH THE BOSS'S SECRETARY. IT MAY BE NECESSARY TO OFFER A LIVE CALF OR A SUMMER INTERN AS AN ANIMAL SACRIFICE.

UNDERSTANDING ACCOUNTING PEOPLE

PEOPLE WHO WORK IN ACCOUNTING DEPARTMENTS OFTEN WORK TWELVE-HOUR DAYS CREATING REPORTS THAT NOBODY CARES ABOUT. THIS GIVES THEM A VERY BAD ATTITUDE. DO NOT ATTEMPT HUMOR AROUND THEM.

ARE YOU THE CLERK WHO RETAINS ALL OF THE BUDGET ANALYSIS RECORDS?

WHAT IF I AM?

THEN I GUESS YOU COULD BE CONSIDERED "ANALYSIS RETENTIVE."

Hee Hee

HE WAS MIGHTY FAST WITH THOSE SCISSORS.

UNDERSTANDING TECHNICAL PEOPLE

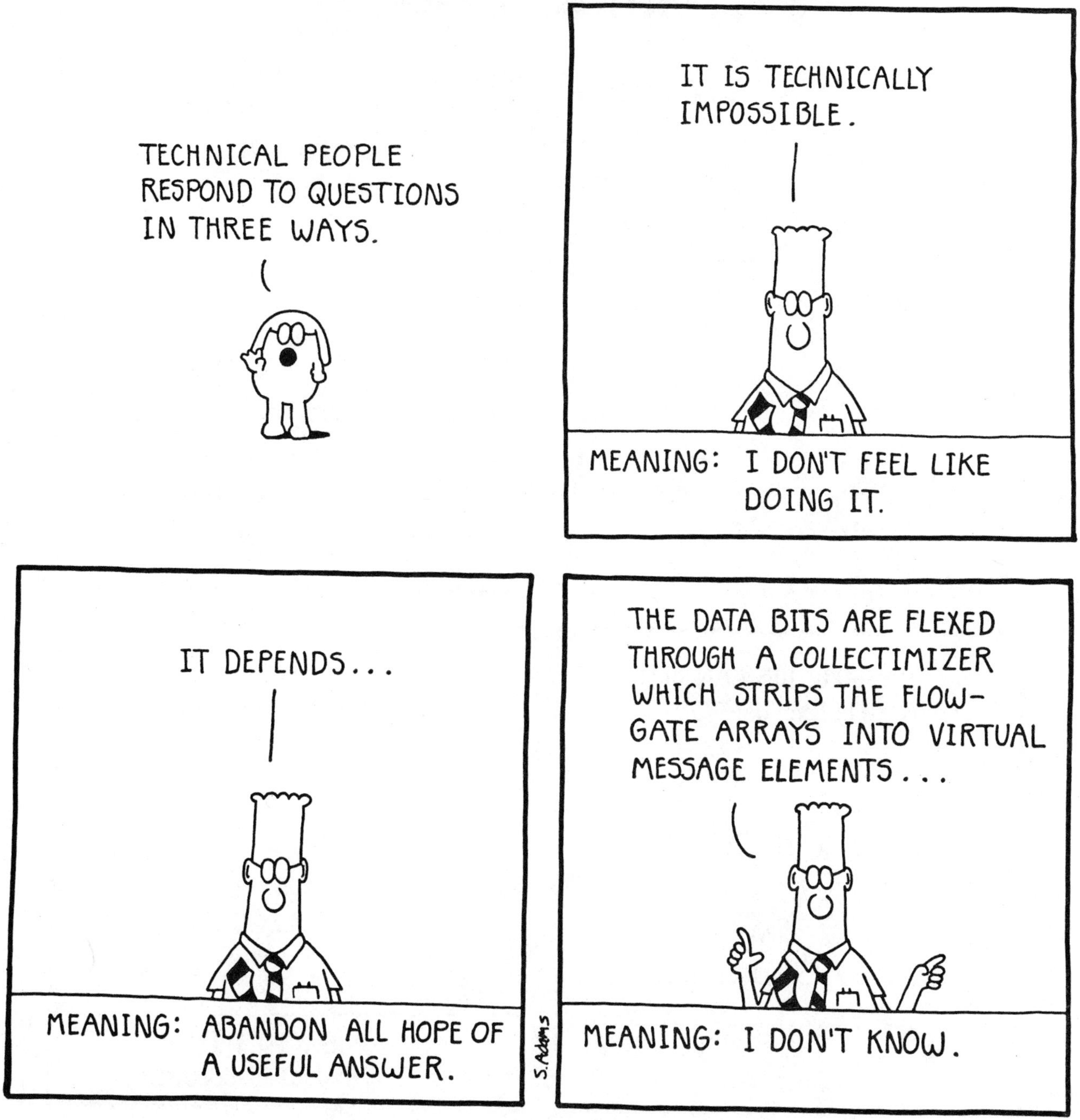
TECHNICAL PEOPLE RESPOND TO QUESTIONS IN THREE WAYS.
IT IS TECHNICALLY IMPOSSIBLE.
MEANING: I DON'T FEEL LIKE DOING IT.
IT DEPENDS...
MEANING: ABANDON ALL HOPE OF A USEFUL ANSWER.
THE DATA BITS ARE FLEXED THROUGH A COLLECTIMIZER WHICH STRIPS THE FLOW-GATE ARRAYS INTO VIRTUAL MESSAGE ELEMENTS...
MEANING: I DON'T KNOW.
S. Adams

MARKETING

TRANSLATING MARKETING TALK

PEOPLE IN MARKETING JOBS ALWAYS SPEAK IN CODE.

OOWA OOWAGA

WE DID EXHAUSTIVE CUSTOMER RESEARCH.

MEANING: I ASKED MY CAT, MITTENS.

I'M SURE WE CAN SELL A MILLION UNITS.

MEANING: YEAH, RIGHT, WHEN PIGS FLOSS.

WE'RE WORKING CLOSELY WITH THE ENGINEERS.

MEANING: WE TOLD THEM OUR FAVORITE COLORS.

UNDERSTANDING MARKETING PEOPLE

PEOPLE ENTER THE MARKETING PROFESSION AFTER THEY REALIZE THAT THEY HAVE GROWN UP WITHOUT ANY PARTICULAR SKILLS.

I SAY WE SHOULD LISTEN TO THE CUSTOMERS AND GIVE THEM WHAT THEY WANT.

WHAT THEY WANT IS BETTER PRODUCTS FOR FREE.

OH... THEN LET'S JUST SELL THEM WHAT WE'VE GOT AND CALL IT A STRATEGY.

PERKS

BUSINESS LUNCHES

WHEN USING THE COMPANY'S MONEY
TO PAY FOR A MEAL, IT IS EXPECTED
THAT YOU WILL ORDER THE MOST
EXPENSIVE ITEMS ON THE MENU.

I'LL HAVE THE
ENDANGERED
SPECIES KABOB.

GIVE ME THE
BIGFOOT SIRLOIN
GRILLED OVER
MOON ROCKS.

S.Adams

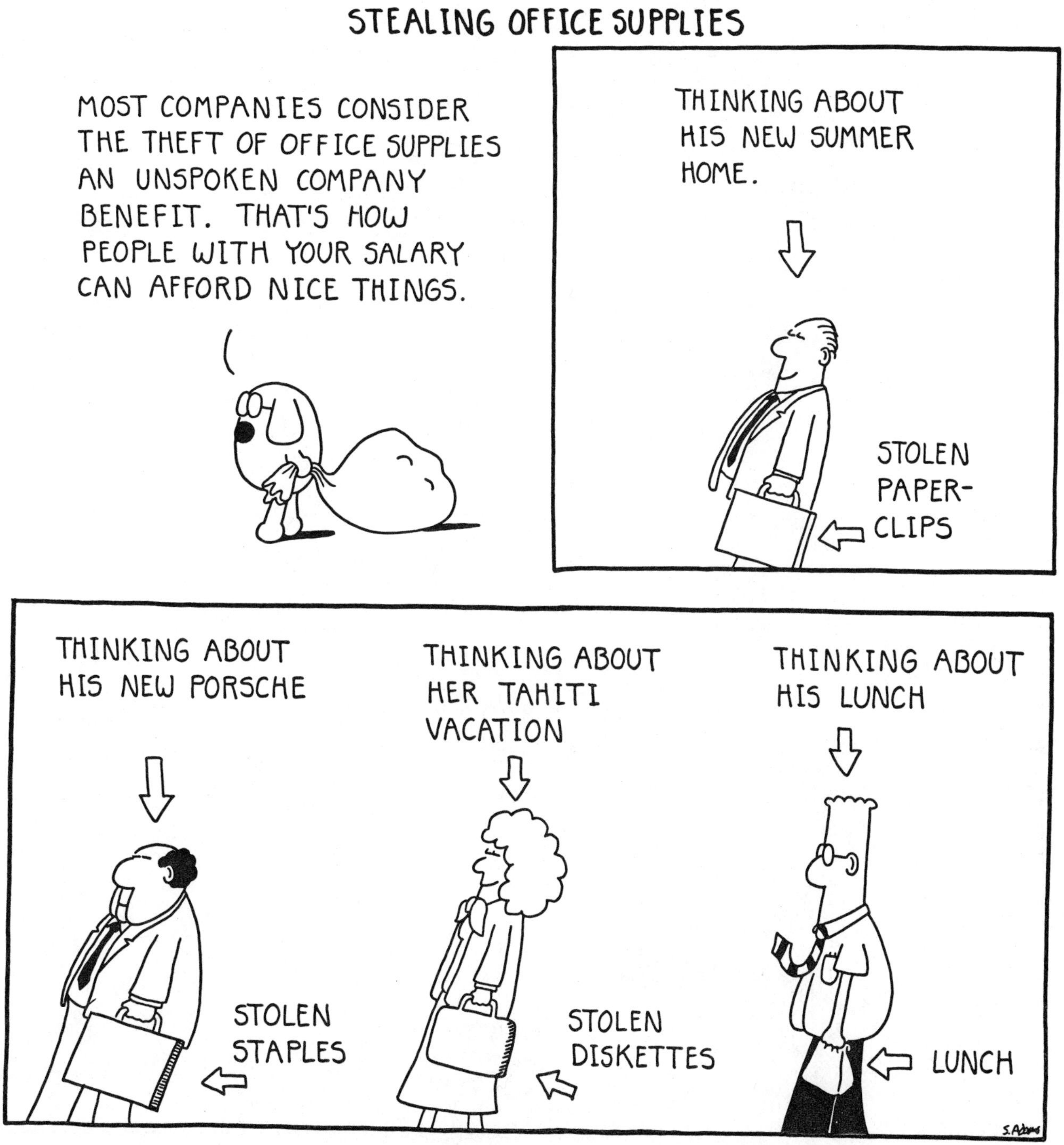
STEALING OFFICE SUPPLIES
MOST COMPANIES CONSIDER THE THEFT OF OFFICE SUPPLIES AN UNSPOKEN COMPANY BENEFIT. THAT'S HOW PEOPLE WITH YOUR SALARY CAN AFFORD NICE THINGS.
THINKING ABOUT HIS NEW SUMMER HOME.
STOLEN PAPER-CLIPS
THINKING ABOUT HIS NEW PORSCHE
STOLEN STAPLES
THINKING ABOUT HER TAHITI VACATION
STOLEN DISKETTES
THINKING ABOUT HIS LUNCH
LUNCH

SICK DAYS

SICK DAYS ARE THE SAME
AS VACATION DAYS, BUT
WITH SOUND EFFECTS.

THE JOY OF FEEDBACK

FEEDBACK IS A BUSINESS TERM WHICH REFERS TO THE JOY OF CRITICIZING OTHER PEOPLE'S WORK. THIS IS ONE OF THE FEW GENUINE PLEASURES OF THE JOB, AND YOU SHOULD MILK IT FOR ALL IT'S WORTH.

THANKS FOR REVIEWING MY REPORT.

IT'S GARBAGE.

I'LL SPRAY PAINT THE REALLY STUPID PARTS.

AND WHAT FLEA MARKET SOLD YOU THAT GOD-AWFUL DRESS?

UNWATCHED PENS

LEGAL OWNERSHIP OF YOUR PEN ENDS WHEN YOU TAKE YOUR EYES OFF OF IT. YOUR CO-WORKERS ARE WAITING FOR ANY OPPORTUNITY TO MAKE IT THEIR OWN.

MEETINGS

USING STEREOTYPES TO SIZE UP A MEETING

YOU CAN USE STEREOTYPES TO RAPIDLY DETERMINE WHO HAS THE MOST POWER AT A BUSINESS MEETING.

RETURNING CALLS DURING A MEETING: MUST BE A MIDDLE MANAGER.

BROUGHT A BAG LUNCH: MUST BE A TECHNICAL PERSON.

HAS NO WRITING MATERIALS: MUST BE A SENIOR EXECUTIVE.

UNAWARE THAT VESTS ARE NOT IN STYLE: MUST BE A BUDGET ANALYST.

TOO MUCH MAKE-UP AND CLEAVAGE: SECRETARY WHO MAY BE HAVING AN AFFAIR WITH AN EXECUTIVE.

TRYING TO LOOK MORE RELAXED THAN ANYBODY ELSE: PROBABLY AN EXECUTIVE.

THE IMPORTANCE OF DONUTS

NEVER CALL A MEETING BEFORE NOON WITHOUT DONUTS OR ALL ORDER WILL BE LOST.

IS IT JUST ME OR IS THERE A DEFINITE LACK OF DONUTS IN THIS MEETING?

I HAVE AN OLD ONE IN MY PURSE, BUT IT'S ONLY FOR EMERGENCIES.

I THINK YOU ATE ALL THE DONUTS YOURSELF.

I SMELLED DONUT ON HIS BREATH.

LOCK THE DOOR...

BUILD A BETTER LIFE BY STEALING OFFICE SUPPLIES   Dogbert's Big Book of Business

DOGBERT'S GROUP I.Q. FORMULA

THE INTELLIGENCE QUOTIENT OF ANY MEETING CAN BE DETERMINED BY STARTING WITH 100 AND SUBTRACTING 5 POINTS FOR EACH PARTICIPANT.

DEALING WITH MEETING BOREDOM

YOU CAN ACTUALLY DIE FROM THE BOREDOM CAUSED BY LONG BUSINESS MEETINGS. THERE ARE THREE BASIC STRATEGIES FOR SURVIVAL:

FANTASIZE

CRACK JOKES

IS THAT YOUR NOSE OR DID A WEASEL CLIMB ON YOUR FACE AND DIE?

GO FOR IT

ZZZZZ

USING MEETINGS TO AVOID WORK

ATTENDING MEETINGS IS CONSIDERED "WORKING" EVEN IF YOU DON'T DO ANYTHING BUT SIT THERE. TRY TO ATTEND AS MANY MEETINGS AS POSSIBLE.

DOGBERT'S RULE OF THREE

NOTHING PRODUCTIVE EVER HAPPENS
WITH MORE THAN THREE PEOPLE IN
A ROOM, BECAUSE SOMEBODY IS
ALWAYS TOO DISTRACTED TO
PARTICIPATE IN A MEANINGFUL WAY.

FRIDAY AFTERNOON MEETINGS

CALENDAR MULTIPLIER EFFECT

IT IS FUTILE TO TRY TO ARRANGE A MEETING WITH MORE THAN THREE PARTICIPANTS. BEYOND THREE IT IS STATISTICALLY IMPOSSIBLE TO FIND A DATE WHEN ALL OF YOU WILL BE AVAILABLE.

THE FIRST TIME EVERYBODY ELSE IS AVAILABLE IS JUNE 8TH IN THE YEAR 3057...

WELL, YEAH, I SUPPOSE YOU WILL BE DEAD BY THEN...

SO I GUESS YOU'LL BE FREE THAT WHOLE DAY.

THE DILBERT DRONE

THE MOST EFFECTIVE WAY TO RESPOND TO A QUESTION IS TO DRONE ENDLESSLY ABOUT UNRELATED TOPICS. THIS HAS THE DUAL ADVANTAGE OF AVOIDING GIVING WRONG ANSWERS AND REDUCING THE VOLUME OF FUTURE QUESTIONS.

WEASEL WORDS, BLUFFING, AND LYING

WEASEL WORDS

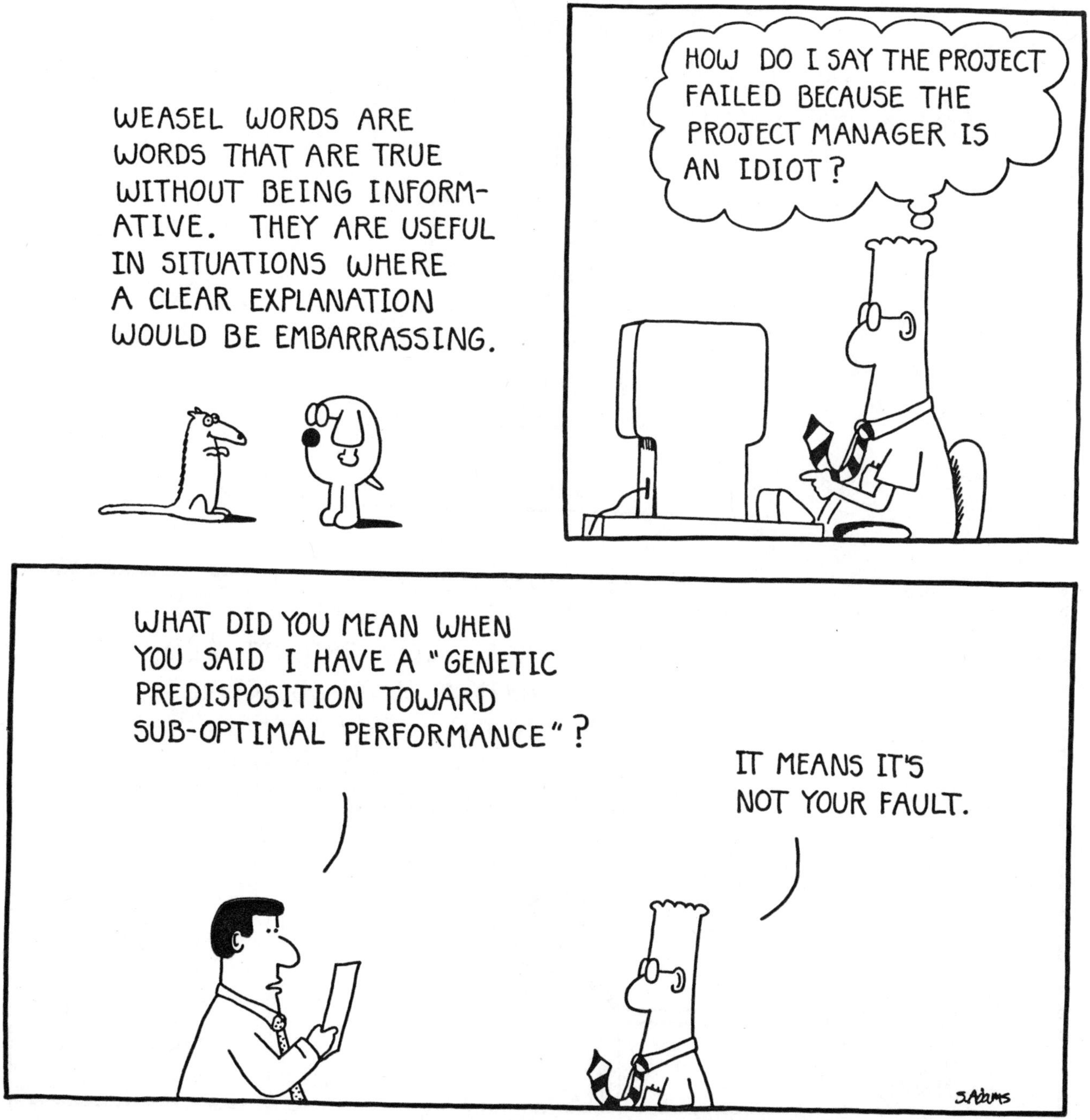
WEASEL WORDS ARE WORDS THAT ARE TRUE WITHOUT BEING INFORMATIVE. THEY ARE USEFUL IN SITUATIONS WHERE A CLEAR EXPLANATION WOULD BE EMBARRASSING.
HOW DO I SAY THE PROJECT FAILED BECAUSE THE PROJECT MANAGER IS AN IDIOT?
WHAT DID YOU MEAN WHEN YOU SAID I HAVE A "GENETIC PREDISPOSITION TOWARD SUB-OPTIMAL PERFORMANCE"?
IT MEANS IT'S NOT YOUR FAULT.
S.Adams

THE VALUE OF BUZZWORDS

BUZZWORDS ARE VALUABLE FOR INTIMIDATING OUT-SIDERS AND MAKING THEM THINK YOU'RE SMARTER THAN YOU REALLY ARE.

DOGBERT

S.Adams

I'M WANTING A JOB.

WE'VE PROACTIVELY PRIORITIZED OUR QUALITY MISSION OBJECTIVES AND REACHED A BREAKTHROUGH STRATEGIC CONCENSUS THAT OUR BOTTOM LINE WOULD BE NEGATIVELY IMPACTED BY THAT PATH FORWARD.

YEAH, AND WE DON'T HIRE PEOPLE WHO TALK FUNNY.

DOGBERT'S RULE OF BUSINESS LIES

VENDORS

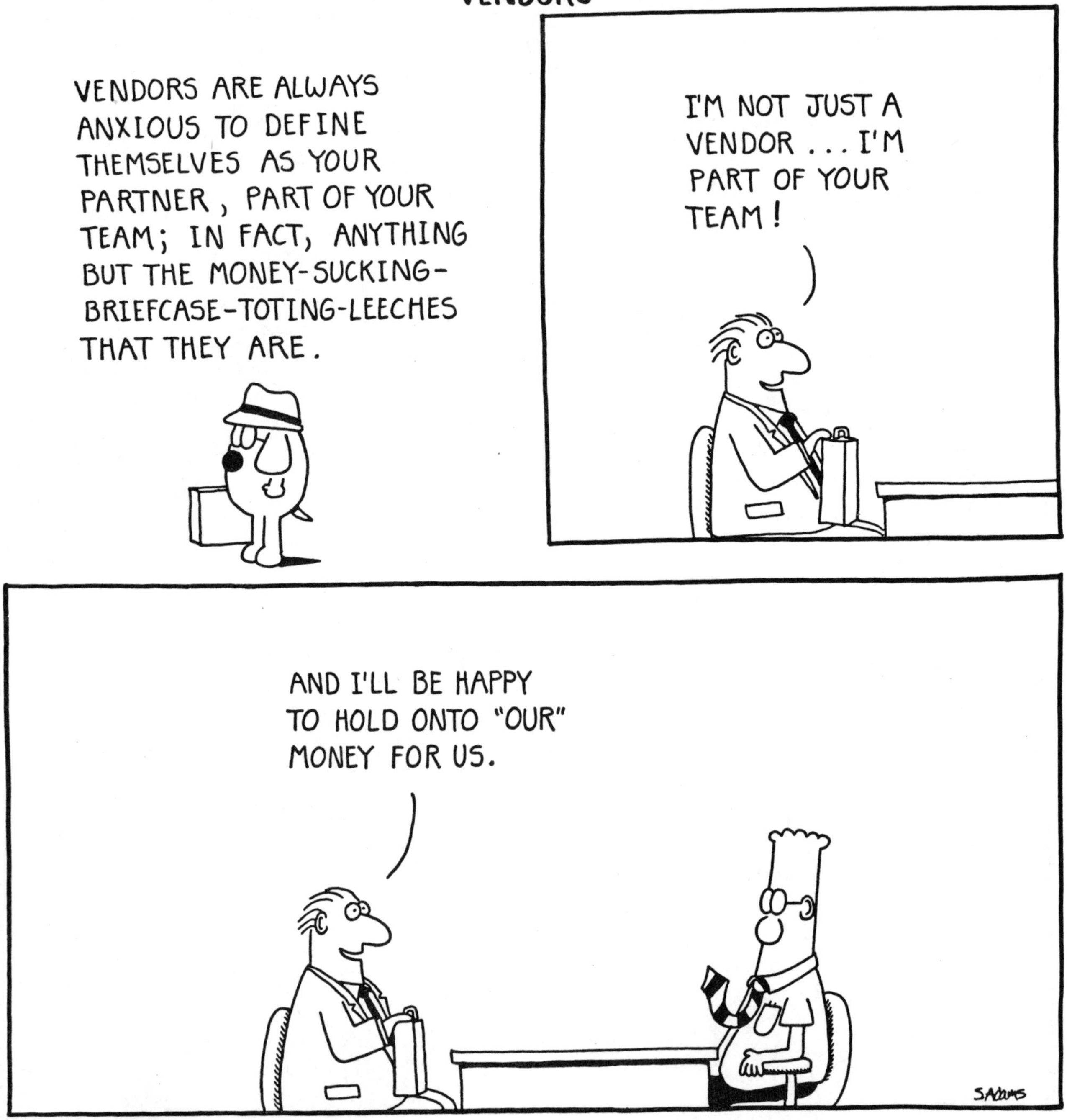
VENDORS ARE ALWAYS ANXIOUS TO DEFINE THEMSELVES AS YOUR PARTNER, PART OF YOUR TEAM; IN FACT, ANYTHING BUT THE MONEY-SUCKING-BRIEFCASE-TOTING-LEECHES THAT THEY ARE.
I'M NOT JUST A VENDOR . . . I'M PART OF YOUR TEAM!
AND I'LL BE HAPPY TO HOLD ONTO "OUR" MONEY FOR US.
S.ADAMS

LYING ON YOUR RÉSUMÉ

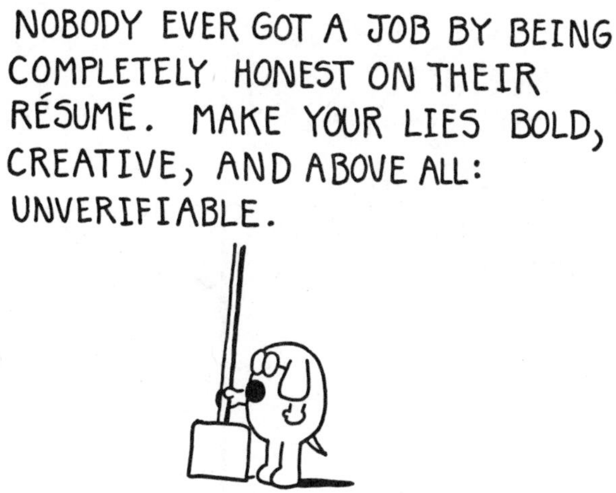
NOBODY EVER GOT A JOB BY BEING COMPLETELY HONEST ON THEIR RÉSUMÉ. MAKE YOUR LIES BOLD, CREATIVE, AND ABOVE ALL: UNVERIFIABLE.

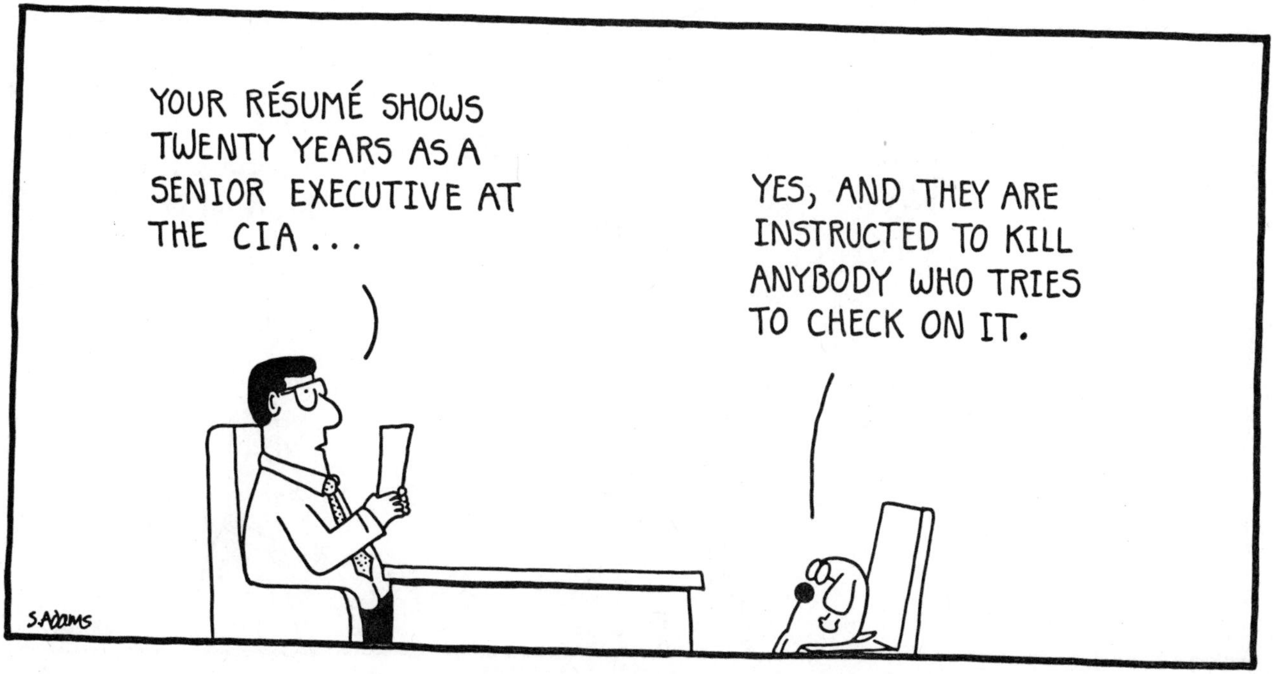
YOUR RÉSUMÉ SHOWS TWENTY YEARS AS A SENIOR EXECUTIVE AT THE CIA . . .
YES, AND THEY ARE INSTRUCTED TO KILL ANYBODY WHO TRIES TO CHECK ON IT.
S.ADAMS

EXCUSES FOR BEING LATE

YOU'RE LATE.

NOBODY GOES TO MEETINGS ON TIME AND NEITHER SHOULD YOU. JUST REMEMBER THAT YOUR EXCUSE MUST BE MORE DRAMATIC THAN THOSE WHO ARRIVE BEFORE YOU.

TRAFFIC WAS TERRIBLE. I THINK THERE WAS AN ACCIDENT.

I WAS THE ACCIDENT. I RAN OVER SOME KIND OF BIG ANIMAL.

SOMEBODY RAN OVER MY MOTHER.

NOBODY KNOWS ANY MORE THAN YOU DO

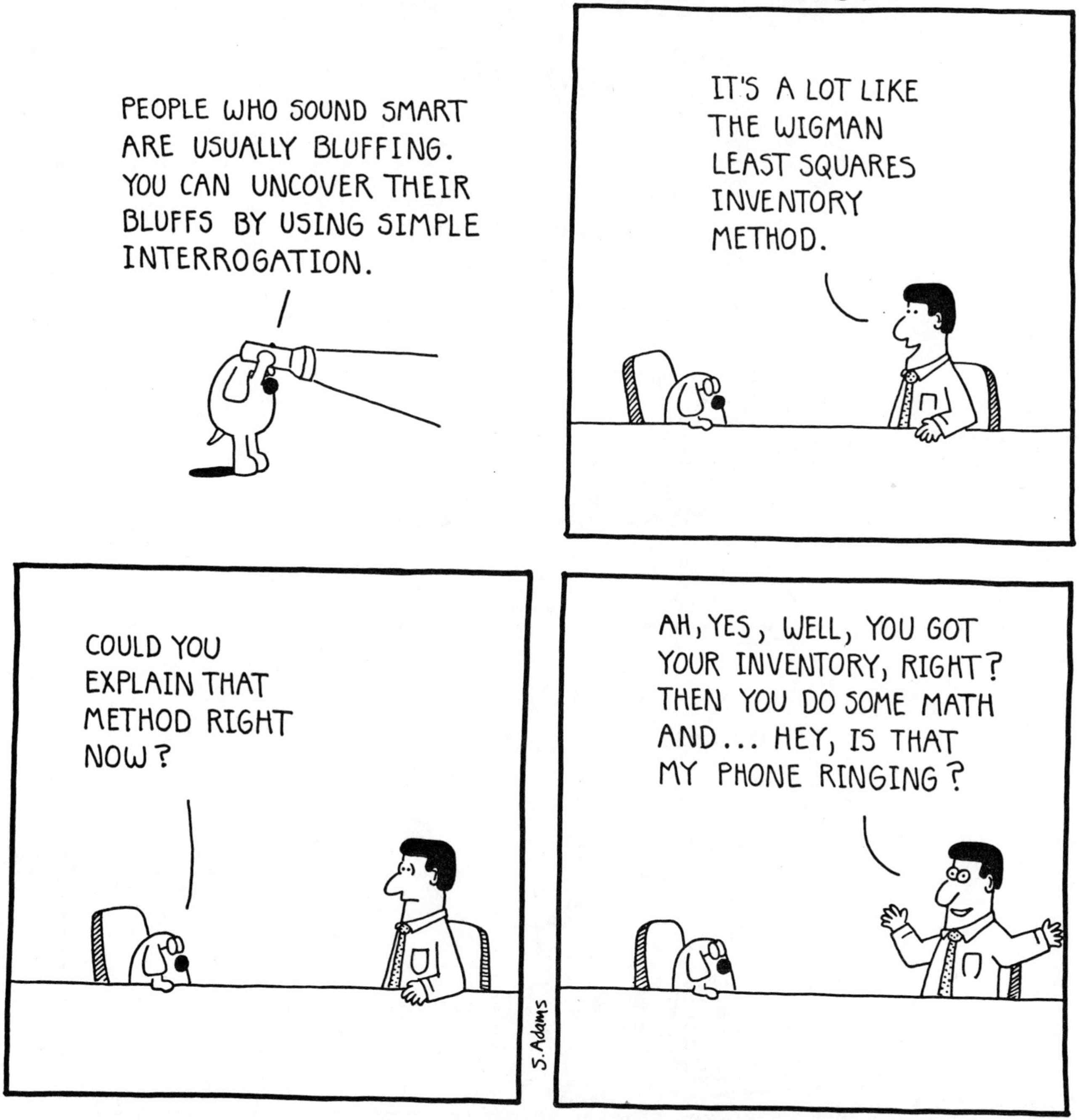
PEOPLE WHO SOUND SMART ARE USUALLY BLUFFING. YOU CAN UNCOVER THEIR BLUFFS BY USING SIMPLE INTERROGATION.
IT'S A LOT LIKE THE WIGMAN LEAST SQUARES INVENTORY METHOD.
COULD YOU EXPLAIN THAT METHOD RIGHT NOW?
AH, YES, WELL, YOU GOT YOUR INVENTORY, RIGHT? THEN YOU DO SOME MATH AND... HEY, IS THAT MY PHONE RINGING?
S. Adams

TECHNOLOGY AND INNOVATION

INNOVATION

COMPANIES ARE GENERALLY SLOW TO ADOPT NEW WAYS OF BUSINESS, ESPECIALLY IF IT MEANS A REDUCTION IN THEIR BELOVED PAPER.

HOW TECHNOLOGY FREES US FROM WORK

TECHNOLOGY HAS MET ITS PROMISE OF REDUCING OUR WORK LOAD. IT DOES THIS PRIMARILY BY PREVENTING US FROM DOING ANY WORK AT ALL.

TELECOMMUTE YOUR WAY TO MORE LEISURE TIME

FOR ONE BRIEF TECHNOLOGICAL WINDOW IN HISTORY, IT IS POSSIBLE TO CLAIM YOU ARE WORKING AT HOME BUT NEARLY IMPOSSIBLE FOR YOUR BOSS TO CHECK ON YOU. YOU SHOULD ARRANGE FOR AT LEAST ONE TELECOMMUTE DAY PER WEEK.

LIE TO YOUR COMPUTER

COMPUTERS HATE PEOPLE. THEY WILL DESTROY YOUR DATA JUST TO BE MEAN. YOUR BEST STRATEGY IS TO LIE TO YOUR COMPUTER AND CONVINCE IT THAT YOU DON'T CARE ABOUT YOUR DATA.

NO IMPORTANT DATA HERE ... NO, JUST A BUNCH OF TRIVIAL WORDS AND NUMBERS THAT I COULDN'T CARE LESS ABOUT ...

HE'S BLUFFING ... I'M GOING DOWN, SUCKER.

s.Adams

ALL PROGRESS IS BASED ON FAULTY ASSUMPTIONS

NOBODY WOULD TRY ANYTHING NEW IF THEY UNDERSTOOD THE CONSEQUENCES. THEREFORE, ALL PROGRESS IS BASED ON FAULTY ASSUMPTIONS.

DOGBERT

EXAMPLE #1

I CALL IT THE "WHEEL" AND IT WILL MAKE CIVILIZATION MUCH LESS COMPLICATED.

REALLY?

EXAMPLE #2

I CALL IT THE "TELEVISION," AND IT WILL BE A BOON TO CULTURE AND EDUCATION.

REALLY?

EXAMPLE #3

I CALL IT A "PERSONAL COMPUTER," AND IT WILL ELIMINATE PAPER WHILE FREEING US ALL FROM TEDIOUS AND UNFULFILLING JOBS.

REALLY?

S.Adams

STYLE VERSUS SUBSTANCE

GREAT IDEAS CAN BE WRITTEN ON GARBAGE

THROUGHOUT HISTORY, MANY GREAT IDEAS STARTED AS SCRIBBLES ON THE BACKS OF ENVELOPES, MATCH BOOKS, AND COCKTAIL NAPKINS. BUT UNLESS YOU'RE PRETTY CONFIDENT ABOUT YOUR IDEA IT IS BEST TO USE REGULAR PAPER WHEN YOU SHOW IT TO THE BOSS.

THIS IS IT? THIS IS YOUR PROPOSAL?

YES SIR, WRITTEN ON THE CORN FLAKES I WAS HAVING WHEN THE IDEA CAME TO ME.

I PROBABLY SHOULDN'T HAVE STAPLED THE PAGES TOGETHER.

THE POWER OF FORMATTING

A WELL-FORMATTED, STUPID PROPOSAL WILL GET FARTHER THAN A GOOD IDEA WHICH IS POORLY FORMATTED.

AT FIRST, I THOUGHT YOUR PROPOSAL WAS RIDICULOUS...

THEN I NOTICED HOW WELL-FORMATTED IT IS, YOUR CREATIVE USE OF ITALICS, THE HIGH QUALITY OF THE PLASTIC COVER... I MUST SAY IT SWAYED ME.

WAIT... WHAT'S THIS LITTLE TWO-DOTTED THING?

IT'S A COLON, SIR. THEY'RE ALL THE RAGE.

ANALYSIS AS A TOOL TO AVOID DECISIONS

THE PURPOSE OF ANALYSIS IS TO AVOID MAKING HARD DECISIONS. THEREFORE, THERE CAN NEVER BE TOO MUCH ANALYSIS.

DID YOU DO A PRESENT VALUE ANALYSIS?

YES.

ENVIRONMENTAL STUDY?

YES

BUDGET ANALYSIS?

YES

STOCKHOLDER IMPACT?

YES

CARBON DATING?

UH...NO

WELL, THEN YOU'RE WASTING MY TIME, AREN'T YOU.

GETTING AWAY WITH IT

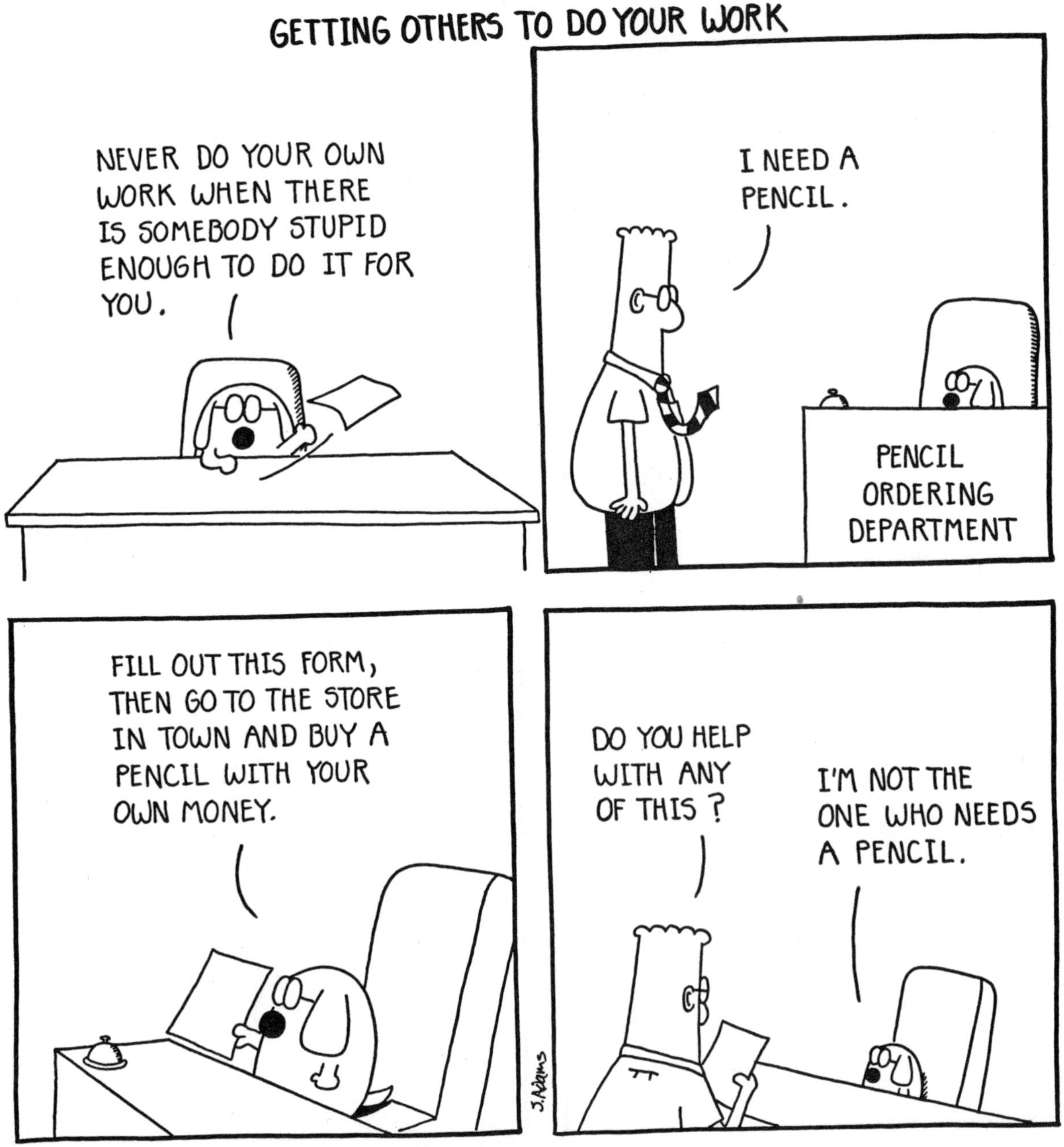
GETTING OTHERS TO DO YOUR WORK
NEVER DO YOUR OWN WORK WHEN THERE IS SOMEBODY STUPID ENOUGH TO DO IT FOR YOU.
I NEED A PENCIL.
PENCIL ORDERING DEPARTMENT
FILL OUT THIS FORM, THEN GO TO THE STORE IN TOWN AND BUY A PENCIL WITH YOUR OWN MONEY.
DO YOU HELP WITH ANY OF THIS?
I'M NOT THE ONE WHO NEEDS A PENCIL.
S. Adams

THE DOGBERT DEFLECTION

WHEN ASKED A QUESTION, NEVER ADMIT THAT YOU DON'T HAVE THE ANSWER. INSTEAD, RESPOND WITH AN IMPOSSIBLE QUESTION OF YOUR OWN.

DOGBERT, DO YOU HAVE THE MONTHLY SALES TOTALS FOR THE BOSS?

YES, OF COURSE. DO YOU WANT IT BY INDUSTRY CODE, ZIP CODE, PRODUCT CODE, GOOMBA CODE, PENAL CODE OR BLAH BLAH CODE?

UH... I DON'T KNOW...

IF YOU DON'T KNOW WHAT YOU NEED, WHY ARE YOU HERE?

AVOIDING CRITICISM

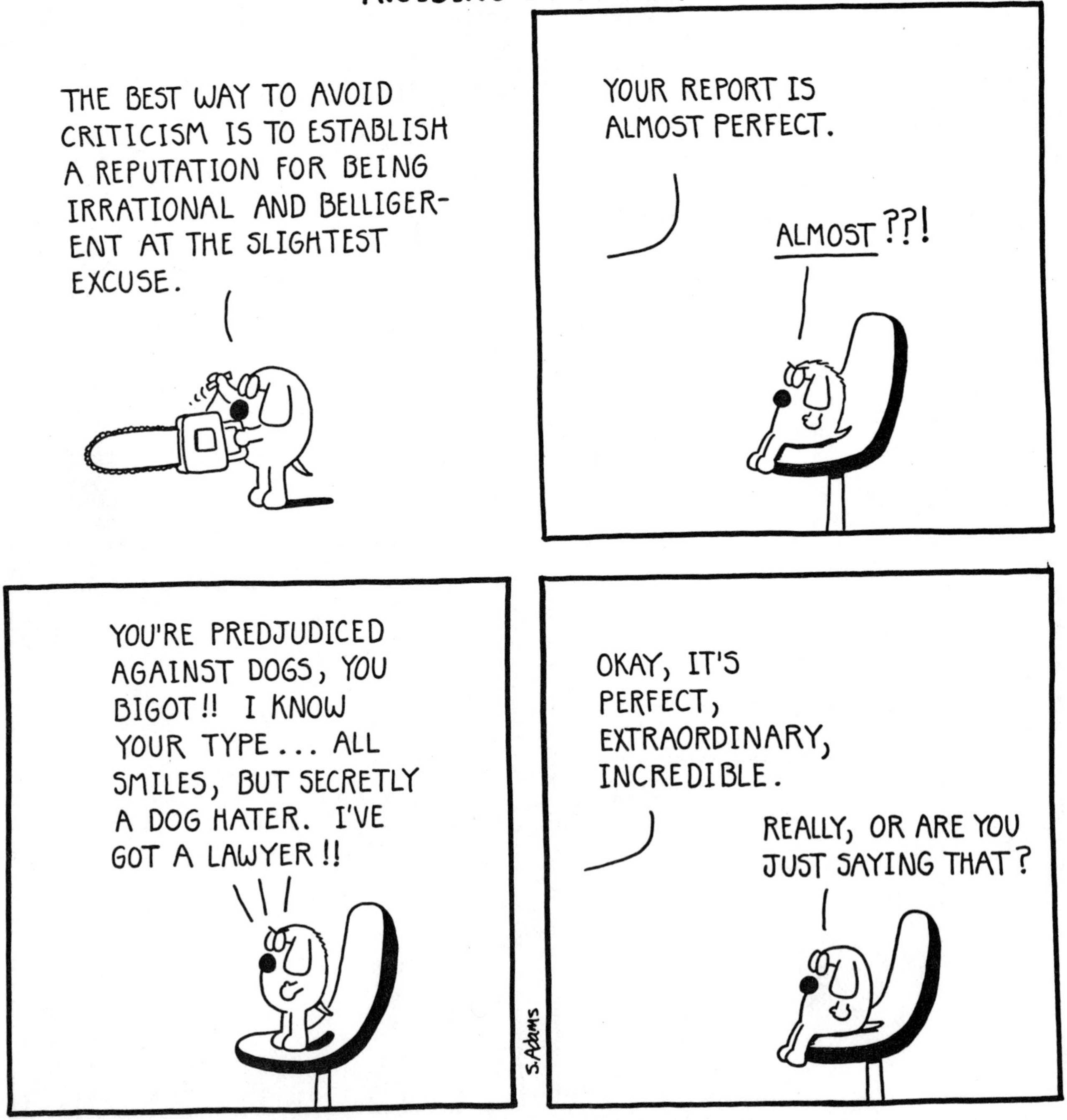
THE BEST WAY TO AVOID CRITICISM IS TO ESTABLISH A REPUTATION FOR BEING IRRATIONAL AND BELLIGERENT AT THE SLIGHTEST EXCUSE.
YOUR REPORT IS ALMOST PERFECT.
ALMOST ??!
YOU'RE PREDJUDICED AGAINST DOGS, YOU BIGOT!! I KNOW YOUR TYPE... ALL SMILES, BUT SECRETLY A DOG HATER. I'VE GOT A LAWYER!!
OKAY, IT'S PERFECT, EXTRAORDINARY, INCREDIBLE.
REALLY, OR ARE YOU JUST SAYING THAT?

HANDLING QUESTIONS

PEOPLE DON'T ASK QUESTIONS TO GET ANSWERS -- THEY ASK QUESTIONS TO SHOW HOW SMART THEY ARE. YOUR BEST STRATEGY IS TO SAY YOU'LL GET BACK TO THEM BUT NEVER DO IT.

HAVE YOU COMPARED YOUR PROPOSAL TO THE TECHNIQUES USED BY ANCIENT ELBYSINIAN SOCIETIES?

GOSH, NO, BUT I'LL RESEARCH IT AND GET BACK TO YOU.

JERK

GETTING FIRED

BIG COMPANIES HAVE PROCEDURES THAT MAKE IT NEARLY IMPOSSIBLE TO FIRE ANYBODY. IF YOU HAVE NO CAREER AMBITION AND NO PRIDE YOU CAN TAKE GREAT ADVANTAGE OF THIS SITUATION.

PRIORITIZING YOUR WORK

YOU CAN TELL HOW IMPORTANT AN ASSIGNMENT IS BY HOW IT IS COMMUNICATED TO YOU.

IN BASKET: TOTALLY UNIMPORTANT. YOU MAY SAFELY IGNORE IT FOREVER.

IN

TELEPHONE: IGNORE IT. NO IMPORTANT ASSIGNMENT HAS EVER BEEN GIVEN OVER THE TELEPHONE.

RRRRING

PERSONAL THREAT: MAKE SOME TIME ON YOUR CALENDAR.

TUESDAY?

S. Adams

DOGMAS

DOGBERT'S THEORY OF DELEGATION

ALL ASSIGNMENTS ARE EVENTUALLY DELEGATED TO THE PERSON WHO UNDERSTANDS THEM THE LEAST.

WRITE A MEMO ON THE PROBLEM WITH THE AZAK PROJECT.

WHAT PROBLEM?

WRITE A MEMO ON THE PROBLEM WITH THE AZAK PROJECT.

WHAT'S THE AZAK PROJECT?

WRITE A MEMO ON THE PROBLEM WITH THE AZAK PROJECT.

WHAT'S A MEMO.

THE IMPORTANCE OF STRATEGIES

PESSIMISM AND JOB EXPERIENCE

AN OPTIMIST IS SIMPLY A PESSIMIST WITH NO JOB EXPERIENCE. PESSIMISM INCREASES STEADILY OVER A CAREER UNTIL THE TENTH YEAR AND THEN REMAINS CONSTANT.

JUST HIRED

GREAT IDEA! LET'S START RIGHT AWAY!

FIVE YEARS EXPERIENCE

WE TRIED THAT IDEA FIVE YEARS AGO. IT DIDN'T WORK THEN AND IT WON'T WORK NOW.

TEN YEARS EXPERIENCE

WE'RE ALL GOING TO DIE ... DIE OR GO TO JAIL ... IT'S THE END OF LIFE AS WE KNOW IT ...

S. ADAMS

THE RIGHT APPROACH

THE CORRECT APPROACH TO ANY SITUATION IS, BY AMAZING COINCIDENCE, THE ONLY APPROACH YOU KNOW.

THIS IS A CLASSIC APPLICATION FOR THE "SWANSON WEIGHTED CASH FLOW ANALYSIS," WHICH I KNOW SO WELL.

NO, NO, WE NEED TO BUILD A COMPUTER MODEL.

BAH! WE JUST NEED TO KICK SOME HINEYS, THAT'S ALL.

LISTEN TO ME, PEOPLE! WE MUST STICK THEM WITH QUILLS — IT'S THE ONLY WAY!

S. Adams

EVOLUTION OF A FACT

WILD GUESSES CAN BE TRANSFORMED INTO BUSINESS FACTS THROUGH THE MIRACLE OF COMMUNICATIONS.

STEP ONE: WILD GUESS

I DUNNO... IT COULD BE ANYWHERE FROM ONE TO A MILLION.

STEP TWO: RUMOR

THEY SAY IT COULD BE A MILLION.

STEP THREE: FACT

EXPERTS SAY ONE MILLION.

RUMORS

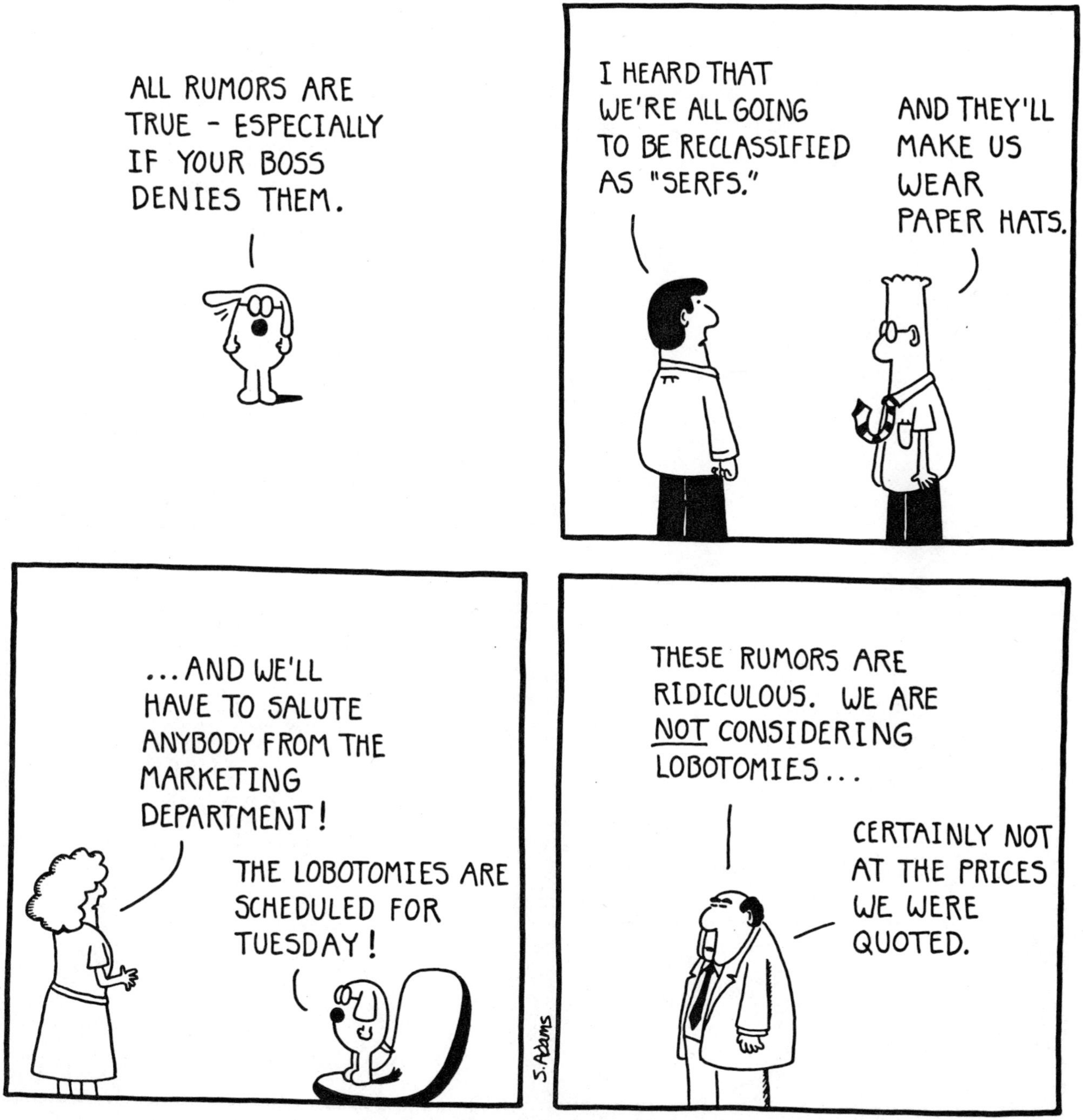
ALL RUMORS ARE TRUE - ESPECIALLY IF YOUR BOSS DENIES THEM.
I HEARD THAT WE'RE ALL GOING TO BE RECLASSIFIED AS "SERFS."
AND THEY'LL MAKE US WEAR PAPER HATS.
...AND WE'LL HAVE TO SALUTE ANYBODY FROM THE MARKETING DEPARTMENT!
THE LOBOTOMIES ARE SCHEDULED FOR TUESDAY!
S. Adams
THESE RUMORS ARE RIDICULOUS. WE ARE NOT CONSIDERING LOBOTOMIES...
CERTAINLY NOT AT THE PRICES WE WERE QUOTED.

DOGBERT'S RULE OF STRATEGIES

ANY GOOD STRATEGY WILL SEEM RIDICULOUS BY THE TIME IT IS IMPLEMENTED.

?

EXECUTIVE OFFICES

LET'S OFFER AN EARLY RETIREMENT INCENTIVE.

YEAH, THAT WAY WE CAN AVOID LAYOFFS.

THE EMPLOYEES WILL UNDER-STAND AND LOVE US.

LOWER MANAGEMENT

WE HAVE TO ROUND UP THE EXPERIENCED EMPLOYEES AND PAY THEM TO LEAVE.

S. Adams

WHAT YOU DO

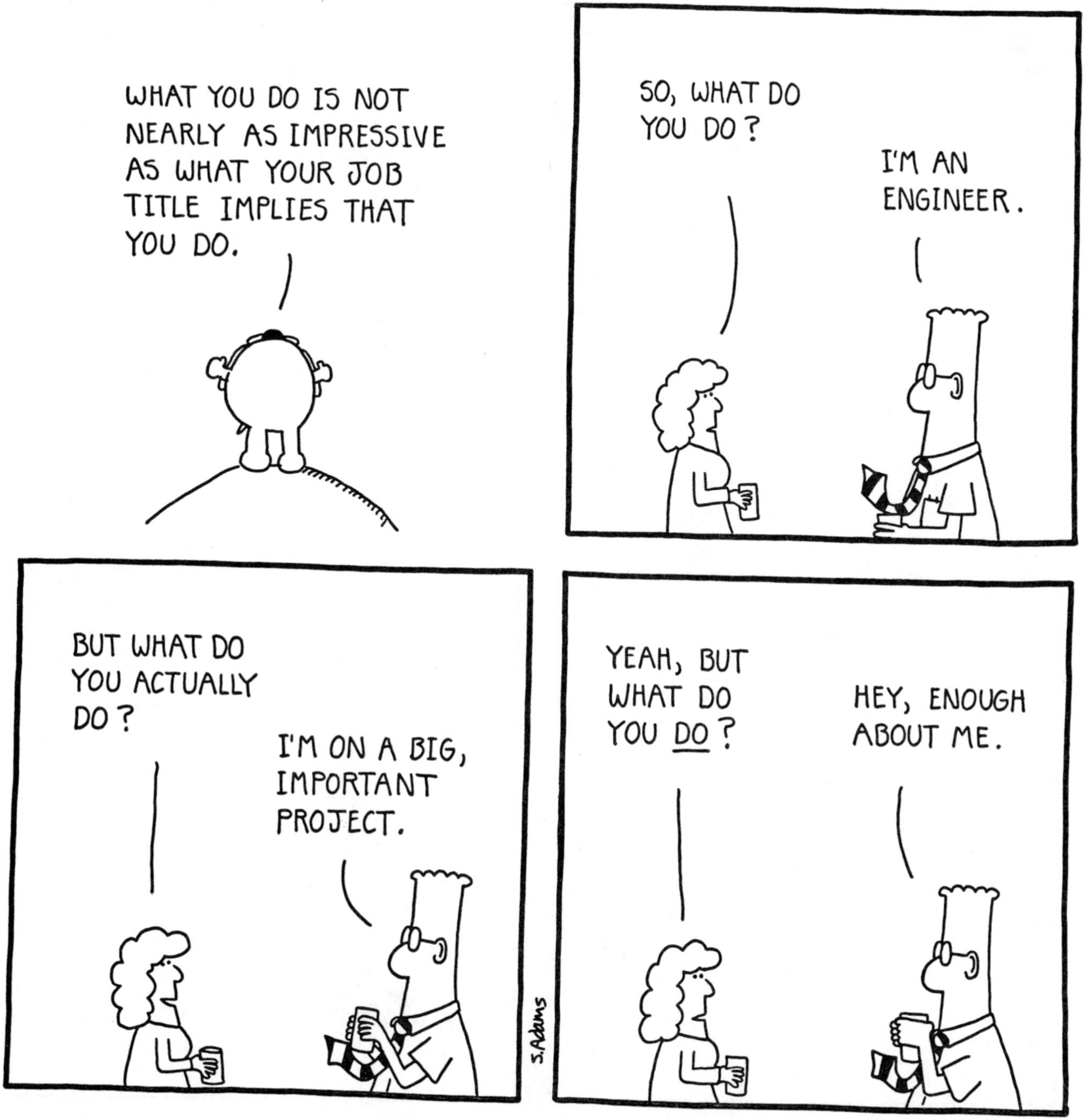

WHAT YOU DO IS NOT NEARLY AS IMPRESSIVE AS WHAT YOUR JOB TITLE IMPLIES THAT YOU DO.
SO, WHAT DO YOU DO?
I'M AN ENGINEER.
BUT WHAT DO YOU ACTUALLY DO?
I'M ON A BIG, IMPORTANT PROJECT.
YEAH, BUT WHAT DO YOU DO?
HEY, ENOUGH ABOUT ME.

HOW TO IDENTIFY AN EXPERT

AN EXPERT IS A PERSON WHO HAS BEEN ASSIGNED TO AN EXPERT'S JOB. NO OTHER QUALIFICATIONS ARE NECESSARY.

DOGBERT'S TIPS

HOW TO MAKE YOUR BORING JOB SOUND DANGEROUS

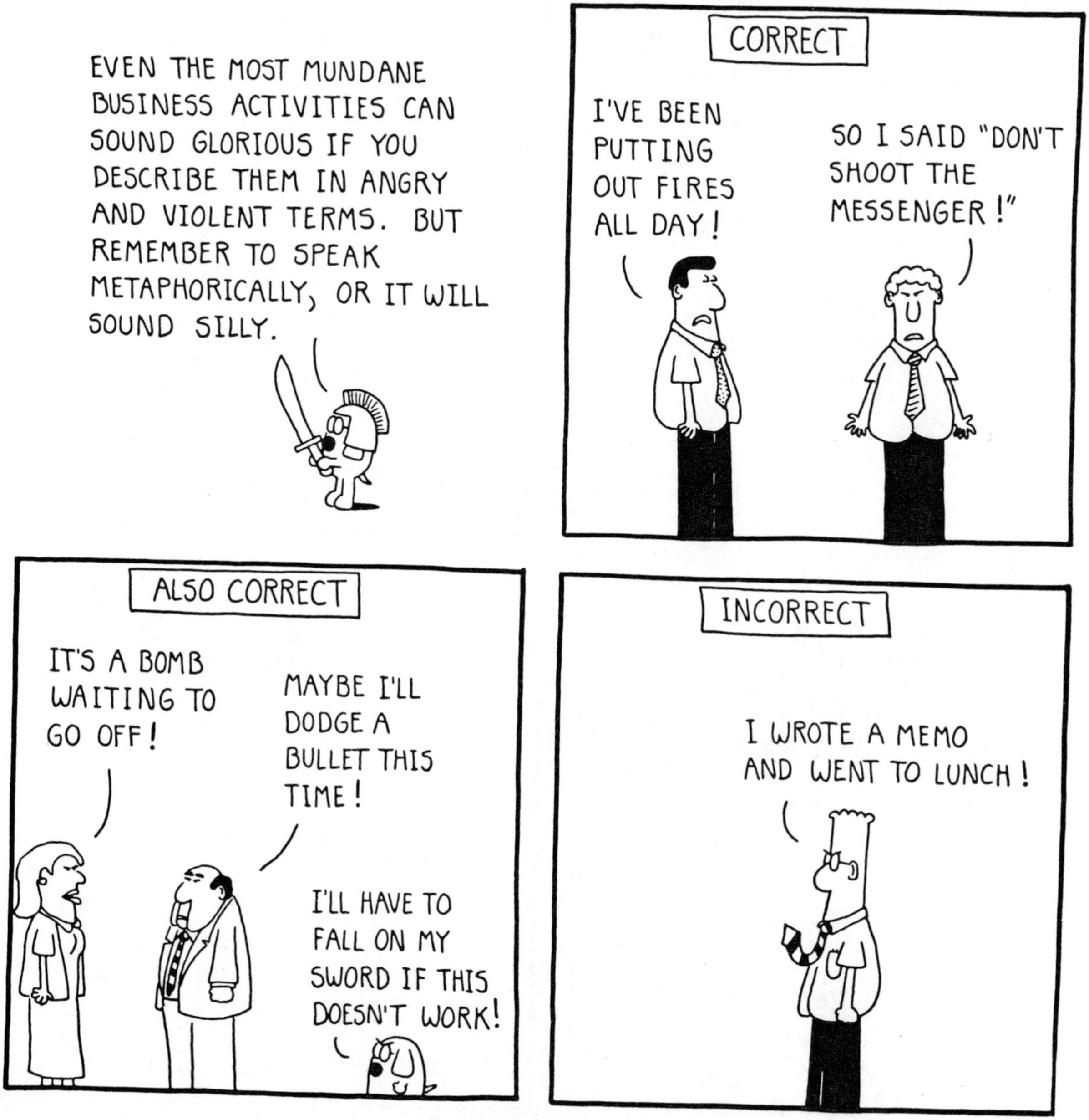
EVEN THE MOST MUNDANE BUSINESS ACTIVITIES CAN SOUND GLORIOUS IF YOU DESCRIBE THEM IN ANGRY AND VIOLENT TERMS. BUT REMEMBER TO SPEAK METAPHORICALLY, OR IT WILL SOUND SILLY.
CORRECT
I'VE BEEN PUTTING OUT FIRES ALL DAY!
SO I SAID "DON'T SHOOT THE MESSENGER!"
ALSO CORRECT
IT'S A BOMB WAITING TO GO OFF!
MAYBE I'LL DODGE A BULLET THIS TIME!
I'LL HAVE TO FALL ON MY SWORD IF THIS DOESN'T WORK!
INCORRECT
I WROTE A MEMO AND WENT TO LUNCH!

WHEN TO CHANGE JOBS

CHANGING JOBS IS A TRAUMATIC AND DEGRADING PROCESS. YOU SHOULD ONLY DO IT WHEN YOUR CURRENT JOB BECOMES UNBEARABLE. FIND YOURSELF ON THIS GUIDE TO HELP YOUR DECISION.

NOT TIME TO CHANGE JOBS YET

START PREPARING A RÉSUMÉ

CONSIDER A JOB CHANGE

KEEPING YOUR PERSPECTIVE

YOUR JOB IS UTTERLY INSIGNIF-
ICANT. BUT ON THE PLUS SIDE,
NOTHING YOU COULD DO WOULD
SERIOUSLY DAMAGE THE PLANET.
DON'T TAKE ANY OF IT TOO
SERIOUSLY.

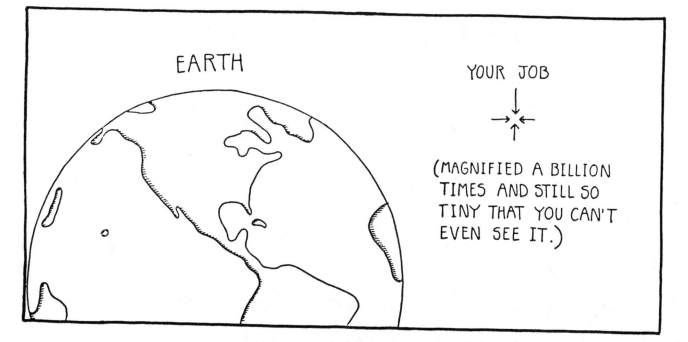

EARTH

YOUR JOB

(MAGNIFIED A BILLION
TIMES AND STILL SO
TINY THAT YOU CAN'T
EVEN SEE IT.)

FUNNY BUSINESS!

You want to stay ahead of the competition, right? Of course right! Then your next job is to acquire these high-quality, low-cost Topper titles...

_____ **ALWAYS POSTPONE MEETINGS WITH TIME-WASTING MORONS**
A Dilbert Book by Scott Adams $7.95

The collected DILBERT comics starting at the strip's debut. A must-have for the dedicated fan!

_____ **BUILD A BETTER LIFE BY STEALING OFFICE SUPPLIES Dogbert's Big Book of Business.**
Illustrated by Scott Adams. $7.95

Dogbert, the entrepreneurial quadruped from the nationally syndicated DILBERT strip, expounds on the world of work.

_____ **FRANK AND ERNEST CAREER ADVICE How to Make Your Job Work for You.**
Tom Greening, Ph.D. Illustrated by Bob Thaves. $7.95

A career counselor/psychotherapist's straightforward advice on workplace problems, punctuated with hilariously insightful FRANK AND ERNEST cartoons.

_____ **TOTAL BOOKS**

Yes, please rush me the above books. My check or money order for _____ is enclosed!
(Please add $1.50 per book for postage and handling. U.S. dollars only. Make check or money order payable to Topper Books.)

Name _____

Address _____

City _____ State _____ Zip _____

Return to Topper Books, United Media, 200 Park Ave., New York, NY 10166. Please allow 4-6 weeks for delivery.